THE OLD SPOT COOKBOOK

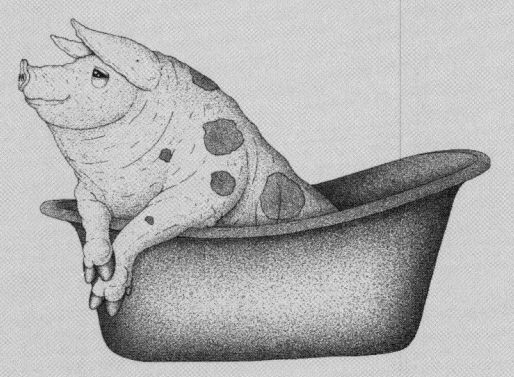

THE OLD SPOT COOKBOOK

A DECADE AT DUBLIN'S FAVOURITE GASTROPUB

AOIFE CARRIGY

NINE BEAN ROWS

CONTENTS

INTRODUCTION 1
OUR TEAM 12
OUR SUPPLIERS 16
DRINKS AT THE OLD SPOT 22
INGREDIENTS, MEASUREMENTS AND TECHNIQUES 24

SNACKS AND STARTERS 28
BROWN BREAD AND SOUP 62
LOW AND SLOW 74
MAINS 90
SIDES 118
SUNDAY ROASTS 124
PIES 138
DESSERTS 150
COCKTAILS 168
PANTRY 190

INDEX 214
ACKNOWLEDGEMENTS 220

INTRODUCTION

ON A QUIET corner in Dublin, under the rail line that connects the Silicon Docks with the city and its seaside suburbs, there's a spotted pig taking a wash in a claw-footed bath.

'Welcome to The Old Spot', the hand-painted sign reads.

Look across the road, down Shaw's Lane, to catch sight of the clean curves of Aviva Stadium putting its own spin on the wide sky's ever-changing light. Cock an ear down Bath Avenue to hear the seagulls call as they wheel out to Irishtown Nature Park, Dublin Port and the Liffey meeting the bay.

Push the door open and step inside through the glass-panelled porch and into the warmth of the front bar: the pub at the heart of our award-winning gastropub.

Welcome to The Old Spot – or 'The Right Spot', as dubbed by Mihaela Hostinariu, who has worked here since 2017 and so speaks with some authority on the matter.

Maybe you're here for a creamy pint or craft beer after a canal-side walk – or a well-made cocktail if that's more your mood. (If you're undecided, our 'cocktail of the week' blackboard special might swing it, or just ask Stephen Kelly or Izzy Conceição behind the bar for their current favourite.) Maybe you want to grab a high stool beside the beer taps and a Wagyu beef burger with beef dripping fries, or a bowl of mussels pil pil with sourdough bread for mopping up that insanely good sauce. Or nab a corner table under one of two walls of windows, where daylight spills onto warm leather banquettes. On overcast days, someone might have lit the candles early to enrich the gleam of all that dark wood. As the light falls outside, the blinds will be dropped halfway down to draw the evening in.

You could happily stay in this room all day, or all night. You could join the locals as they pick their way through sleeping dogs sprawled across the wooden floor. Or you could head on through to the dining room proper, past the reception desk where an army of wine carafes stand ready for action, and Denise McBrien or one of her team are waiting to seat you.

'MY FAVOURITE PLACE IN ALL MY YEARS IN HOSPITALITY IS WORKING THE BAR SECTION ON A BUSY FRIDAY NIGHT WHEN WE'VE LOADS OF DOGS IN. IT'S JUST THE BEST CRAIC. IT'S CARNAGE BUT THE FUN AND ENTERTAINMENT ARE PRICELESS. I ALWAYS HAVE MY BACK POCKET FULL OF TREATS AND THE DOGS ARE FAIRLY QUICK TO PICK UP ON IT, WHICH GUARANTEES THE WELCOME I GET AT THE TABLE. STACK THAT ON TOP OF ALL THE CUSTOMERS LOVING THE FOOD, DRINK AND ATMOSPHERE, AND THAT'S MY HAPPY PLACE.'

CIARAN KEEGAN, WAITER

Back in 2017, when we were still a young pup of a three-year-old gastropub, one restaurant critic described this space as 'a lovely room, a good balance of relaxed and dignified', admiring the 'vintage maps from New York City and ink drawings from Dublin University sports days dating back to the 1800s'. Seven years on, those walls continue to be fine-tuned by our team, with Jane Palmer their chief curator.

An old friend of owners Brian O'Malley and Stephen Cooney, Jane came on board in The Old Spot's earliest days as marketing and events manager, working alongside then-manager Conor Kavanagh (who has since established his own hospitality management consultancy, Agus Victuals) and later with our general manager, Denise McBrien, to develop the potential of our airy second-floor space for hosting private events. Jane's official role has since evolved into photography and content creation, but her unofficial role as chief curator of those walls is undisputed.

Those verdant landscapes evoking happy cows milling in lush fields are painted by her father, Patrick Palmer, a former graphic designer whose work includes iconic posters and merchandise for everyone from Bruce Springsteen to Madonna. Several more paintings in the building are by her mother, Pamela Silin-Palmer, a talented decorative artist and children's book illustrator who also painted our Old Spot pig in a bath outside.

Jane's favourite print, *Mr Fox's Hunt Breakfast on Xmas Day*, complete with mounted dogs' heads and tables laden with champagne and roast birds, was found in an antique shop. It captures the spirit of the champagne breakfast that The Old Spot staff share every Christmas Eve before we open for one last pre-Christmas service.

After the low-ceilinged cosiness of the downstairs rooms, the space upstairs is an airy surprise. Two handsome adjoining rooms with exposed brick walls, warm wooden tables and dark bentwood chairs are washed with natural light from generous skylights. By evening, the room is backlit by the glow of the open kitchen where head chef Mark Ahessy, sous chef

> **'THE STAFF CHRISTMAS BREAKFAST AT THE OLD SPOT IS A WHOLE BIG THING. EVERYONE GETS TO WORK IN A CHRISTMAS MOOD, WE EXCHANGE PRESENTS AND HAVE A NICE MEAL PREPARED BY THE KITCHEN AND SIT ALL TOGETHER AT A LARGE TABLE LIKE A BIG FAMILY.'**
>
> IARA KELLY, SOUS CHEF

> 'WE'RE ALL RUGBY FANS AROUND HERE. WE'D KNOW EVERYTHING THERE IS TO KNOW ABOUT IT.'
>
> LOCAL RESIDENT LINDA 'MAY' MCMAHON, AKA 'THE MAYORESS' OF BATH AVENUE, AND A REGULAR AT THE BATH AND THE OLD SPOT

'IT'S THAT FAMILY OUTSIDE OF HOME, MORE THAN CO-WORKERS. IT'S ALWAYS COOL TO COME TO WORK.'

GABO VALLES, BARMAN/FLOOR STAFF

Lukasz Maslowski and their happy colleagues are hard at work.

Private parties here give you ringside views into the open kitchen, the beating heart of our gastropub action. Alongside the corporate events now hosted here every week, we have also become a family favourite, hosting engagements, weddings, christenings and beyond. One special recent event was a memorial lunch for Terry Stewart, who had grown up on Bath Avenue and married his beloved Joy in the local church. Terry passed away during the pandemic, so in the summer of 2023, with all restrictions lifted, his family hosted a lunch in The Old Spot in his memory. His daughter, Ali Hewson, and her husband, Bono, were among the guests who enjoyed our roast chicken and fish 'n' chips that day.

Part of what makes this room special is its window-side views. From one corner, you can look down Shaw's Lane to the gleaming Aviva Stadium and down Bath Avenue to The Bath Pub, the original big sister to The Old Spot and their sibling Loyola Group operations in Ireland and Portugal.

When Brian O'Malley acquired Murray's Bar and Lounge in 2012, he initially brought Stephen Cooney on board for legal advice. The pair soon became business partners and worked hard – and hands on – to transform Murray's into The Bath while preserving its community spirit.

When its nearest neighbouring pub, The Lansdowne, came up for sale in 2014, the pair snapped it up to open it as The Old Spot (initially in partnership with brothers Paul and Barry McNerney from Juniors and Paulie's Pizza). They looked to The Spotted Pig in New York as inspiration for the kind of gastropub that they wanted to create: one that gives equal weight to its function as both a proper pub and a gastronomic destination.

Stephen is proud that nothing about The Old Spot suggests that we are part of a pub group. The trick that he and Brian have developed is to find strong leaders in each operation and to let them do what they do best: lead.

> 'THE OLD SPOT WORK ENVIRONMENT IS UNMATCHED. THE EMPLOYEES ARE REALLY GENEROUS AND WILLING TO HELP THROUGH THICK AND THIN. THEY ALL HELPED ME AFTER I SUFFERED A ROBBERY. I FELT LIKE I COULD COUNT ON THEM AT ALL TIMES. WE ARE A FAMILY.'
>
> CARLOS JIMENEZ, FLOOR STAFF

Local resident Linda 'May' McMahon has lived on or just off Bath Avenue for over 50 years and has socialised in The Bath (and Murray's before it) for most of those years. 'Murray's is where we all went,' she says. 'The Lansdowne was a bit more of an auld fellas' pub, but Murray's was a real family pub. Lots of the local women had their regular seats that you wouldn't dare sit in, or not for long anyway. We'd have the best sing-songs and on sunny days we'd chase the sun across the street with our stools.'

She says that Brian and Stephen 'started off on the right foot with The Bath neighbours'. They supported community events, hosted OAP nights for the local folks to eat for free and generally made the locals as welcome as the tech workers from nearby Google, Facebook and X and the rugby crowd from the Aviva Stadium (which reopened in 2010). Key to their success, Linda reckons, is that they 'made good staff pickings' with their 'hugely popular' general managers, Brendan Waldron at The Bath and Denise at The Old Spot. 'They'd do anything for you.'

The area has changed massively since Linda's childhood on the street. 'Our family were one of the first people to have a phone on the street,' she remembers. 'The neighbours would all be queueing to get a call to our house from their relatives in England.'

With neighbouring families of up to a dozen kids each, there were always gangs of local kids to play with. 'It was the best childhood. There were no TVs, no iPads and there were no cars either, or very few, so we had the run of the street.'

If it rained, they'd pile into the public phone box for shelter, checking for any forgotten coins or gaming the AB button for whatever it might release and then running up to Cullen's or Pat Lynch's grocery shops to spend their bounty on penny sweets.

'It's still a brilliant area to live in,' says Linda, who welcomes all the recent changes to the neighbourhood. 'I love all the new businesses and the new people moving in. They're friendly, they run their businesses well and are conscious of residents, especially on match days.'

> **'I'LL NEVER FORGET HOW ALL THE TEAM HELPED ME OUT IN MY DIFFICULT TIME AFTER A MOTORCYCLE ACCIDENT. THEY'RE MY SECOND FAMILY.'**
>
> LUKASZ MASLOWSKI, SOUS CHEF SINCE 2015

'I LOVE CHRISTMAS IN THE OLD SPOT. I ALWAYS DRESS UP AND GO AROUND GETTING THE KIDS READY FOR SANTA.'

TALIE 'THE ELF' SONODA (WHO ALSO MOONLIGHTS AS A FLOOR MANAGER)

On those match days, this quiet corner of Dublin transforms like no other and The Old Spot is the place to have a booking. If you can snag one, you'll be in good company. Everyone is here, from the most regular of regulars to the city's best restaurateurs (and their chefs who have managed to book the day off) to former players on Ireland's rugby team, aka the All Blacks of Europe. Everybody knows everybody, and everybody's cheering for the same team.

Match days are almost as busy as our weekly Sunday roasts, which have become an institution worth travelling across the city for. Luckily, the nearby DART line means that it's not just the Beggars Bush locals who can indulge in the cocktails and fine wines that are as much a part of Sundays here as the roasts themselves.

Don't be surprised to spot lots of our team in here on their days off. General manager Denise and her partner Cathal come for the mussels pil pil with a bottle of Andre Bonhomme Viré-Clessé from Burgundy, or a côte de boeuf blackboard special with a bottle of Vietti Perbacco Nebbiolo from Langhe in Piedmont. (A barrister by profession, Cathal moonlights as The Old Spot's unofficial handyman some days and official doorman on match days; it helps that he knows all our regulars.)

Brian and his wife Nina regularly tuck into the Sunday roast while their four young kids make themselves at home. Head chef Mark and his partner Aga travel in from Wicklow for what they know is the best steak and chips in town. Bartenders or servers perch on the off-duty side of the bar, tucking into a midweek burger and chatting to their regulars.

'We have the best regulars,' Denise says, 'way too many to mention them all by name, but we would be lost without them. During covid they bought gift vouchers, hampers and even online wine tastings to help us keep our lights on.'

Some are regulars for a short season, such as American actors filming in Ireland who adopt us as their home-from-home local. Some come for the match day buzz, then come back again and again. (Yes, that's Brian O'Driscoll and Andy Farrell making themselves at home.) Some are lifetime regulars and have strong opinions on any changes we make to their favourites on the menu. We even have regular dogs who we all know and love.

They all treat The Old Spot like an extension of their own home as much as their favourite local restaurant. We all do. And we hope that you do too.

OUR TEAM

DENISE MCBRIEN
GENERAL MANAGER

'A GREAT SHIP run by the best captain' is how waitress Natalie Keegan neatly sums up The Old Spot under Denise's leadership. 'Being able to be myself and feeling appreciated' is what waitress Annmarie Smith loves about working with Denise. 'There is such a sense of community and family here,' says manager Hazel Higgins. 'You are made to feel like an integral part of the team from the moment you start.'

Denise's assured leadership of 'the happiest front-of-house team around' is commented on by restaurant critics and saw her named Best Restaurant Manager in Ireland at the Irish Restaurant Awards 2023, four years after The Old Spot won Best Gastropub in Ireland.

'I absolutely love it here in The Old Spot,' Denise herself says. In 2023, she celebrated a significant birthday here with her closest friends, her partner Cathal and her family – including her eldest son Conan, who used to work here before moving to Manchester, and her teenage sons Luc and Alex, who work as food runners in The Old Spot. 'I couldn't think of anywhere more special to have that celebration.' Guests ate luxurious fish 'n' chips (turbot, if you don't mind, steamed inside the crispest batter), drank fine wine and cocktails, and danced into the night.

Denise loves everything about The Old Spot. 'I love having a team of such professional waiters,' she says. 'I love the sense of community and I love that I have the freedom to run it like my own business.' She also has the professional capability, having run restaurants such as Pichet, which she co-owned, and Old Street in Malahide, which she set up.

When Denise came to The Old Spot in 2018, she brought long-standing relationships with her: with the best wine and food suppliers, with the most discerning of corporate clientele and a gold dust sprinkling of celebrities too (yes, that's Louis Walsh in the corner). She also brought decades of experience in various aspects of the business.

After an early start as a lounge girl, Denise fell in love with food and fine dining while working at The Tea Room in The Clarence Hotel, where chef Michael Martin had returned from the three-starred Nico's in London. She worked at Cooke's Cafe when it was Dublin's hottest booking, in Peacock Alley when Conrad Gallagher got his first Michelin star and in London with Marco Pierre White when he was changing all the rules.

In another life, Denise might herself have become a chef – and says it's no coincidence that so many of her friends today are chefs. Instead, she added that love of food and uncompromising standards to the front-of-house expertise that she brought to restaurants like Chapter One, L'Ecrivain (where she first worked with our head chef, Mark Ahessy) and Bentley's, which she helped Richard Corrigan set up on St Stephen's Green.

Denise's passion for wine was honed in those same restaurants and during a happy spell working with wine importer Simon Tyrrell. It can be seen in the unique wine list that she has helped craft here at The Old Spot, together with owner Stephen Cooney, who loves finding treasures at wine auctions, and it can be seen in the value she places on regular wine training and tastings for staff.

Ultimately, for all her professional skills and food and beverage knowledge, it is Denise's innate sense of hospitality that makes her the best at what she does. 'I love creating memories with and for people,' she says, 'and I love going out of my way to ensure they have a great time.'

That might mean bringing someone a newspaper if they're waiting on their own. Or it might mean asking the kitchen to cut up the fish of the day into bite-sized pieces for one treasured regular who recently had a stroke, then piece it all back together again so it looks perfect and so she doesn't need her husband's help (and so that he gets some time off too).

Denise will always go the extra mile to look after her staff too. When server Carlos Jimenez's home was robbed, they took cash but also his brand new Calvin Klein underwear. His fellow floor staff chipped together a generous percentage from their tips to ensure Carlos had some cash to spend when he got home to Mexico – but it was Denise, in full 'momager' role, who went into Brown Thomas to buy him replacement pants.

'I want people to feel minded,' Denise says, 'like they would be at a family friend's home.' The resulting atmosphere is infectious. As floor manager Bríd O'Neill describes it, 'It usually doesn't even feel like work. It feels like we've invited loads of guests to a dinner party we're hosting and we're just there to make sure the guests are having fun.'

Look around you the next time you're in with us at The Old Spot and you'll see how Denise and her team do that in style.

MARK AHESSY
HEAD CHEF

CONFIDENT, PRECISE AND upbeat: that's how food critics have described the cooking by our head chef Mark Ahessy here at The Old Spot. That confidence is well earned and the precision has been well honed over a career that has brought him from the gastronomic honeypot of Kenmare to top Michelin kitchens to barrel cooking over live fire on a remote ranch in Nevada.

Mark brings an upbeat energy to all that he does. That translates into a happy kitchen described by another Old Spot chef, Beatriz Favaro, as 'absolutely my favourite place to be', where a busy Sunday roast service for over 400 people is delivered while 'laughing and dancing and enjoying ourselves, because that's who we are: people who like to be here and feel the energy from the customers happily eating their food that was so carefully prepared'.

A magpie of a chef, Mark has gathered skills, techniques and lessons from an unusually broad range of kitchens. Classically trained in some of Ireland's best, he got his first taste of fine dining with chef Bruce Mulcahy of Kenmare (where he also did a season at Sheen Falls) and was sous chef for the legendary Michael Clifford in Clonmel. In Dublin, he has worked with chef and mentor Stephen Gibson at Pichet, has cooked on the meat section in L'Ecrivain, and fish at Chapter One.

It was in his hometown of Clonmel that he first had his culinary curiosity piqued, when the Ballymaloe House-trained chef Tim Phelan became a neighbour and showed a teenage Mark how to flash-cook squid, roll fresh pasta and make his own ice cream. Mark later returned to Clonmel to open The Stonehouse Restaurant, which earned a Michelin Guide listing within six months. He has been head chef in Hang Dai, 777 and Taste by Dylan McGrath, adding Chinese, Mexican and Japanese influences to his eclectic culinary repertoire, along with a stint at Tiller & Grain mastering modern plant-led food and sustainable cooking.

Mark has been head chef at The Old Spot since 2022 and we're lucky to have him. When he's not in the kitchen, you'll find Mark in his music studio, producing psychedelic music under his moniker of Meerkat, or DJing at international dance festivals.

AOIFE CARRIGY
FOOD AND DRINKS WRITER

WITH A GRANDMOTHER who ran the canteen at the Irish Hospitals' Sweepstakes, a mother who studied institutional catering at Cathal Brugha Street (and loved to throw a good party) and siblings who all worked in restaurants from their teen years on, Aoife caught the hospitality bug early.

A Transition Year work experience as commis chef in their favourite family-occasion restaurant, The Wishbone in Glasthule, not only taught Aoife how to segment oranges at speed, but more importantly led to her first waitressing job. For the next 15 years, Aoife had the best times working front of house in some of Dublin's busiest, buzziest restaurants, from De Selby's and Pierre Victoire to La Stampa and Cooke's Cafe to Eden and Bang Café. She used the flexibility and skills afforded by the job to backpack around Europe, the Pacific Islands, Antipodeans and South-East Asia and to intern in publishing houses back home and write restaurant review columns, first for *Dublin Event Guide* and then *Totally Dublin*, before swapping her apron and wine opener for pen and paper as a full-time food, drinks and travel writer.

Aoife worked for five years at Ireland's *Food&Wine Magazine* as deputy to editors Ernie Whalley, Hugo Arnold and Ross Golden-Bannon while studying for her WSET Level 2 and 3 certificates in wine and spirits education. Since 2010, she has freelanced as an editor and journalist, writing for various Irish publications, currently as wine and drinks columnist with the *Irish Independent*. She was general editor of four books for the Irish Countrywomen's Association and has co-authored three restaurant cookbooks, including *Cornucopia: The Green Cookbook* (Gill Books, 2019) which won the An Post Cookbook of the Year 2019, as well as *The Ard Bia Cookbook* (Atrium Press, 2012) and now this special book with The Old Spot.

When Aoife scored her hat trick of three awards in a row from the Irish Food Writing Awards – in 2021 for wine writing, in 2022 for drinks writing and in 2023 for food writing – it felt fitting to celebrate with a Sunday roast at The Old Spot, together with great friends she met through working in great Dublin restaurants. Her favourite memory of that lunch is of floor manager Talie Sonoda guiding the table through their cocktail order while bouncing a baby on her hip, borrowed from the neighbouring table where the young parents looked happy and relaxed. Denise had clocked off at that stage, yet you wouldn't know it: her team deliver seamless service whether she's in the building or not.

Aoife loved working in bars and restaurants. 'I know the pleasure that can be had from looking after people,' she says, 'and of being part of a strong team who are willing to work hard and have fun, doing so thanks to a support system that works. That takes a lot of attention to detail. It's been nothing but a pleasure to work on this cookbook and watch The Old Spot family in action.'

OUR SUPPLIERS

OUR MEATS

RIDGEWAY WAGYU

We take our burgers seriously, so we buy them from the best.

John Corrigan of Ridgeway Wagyu is a neighbour of head chef Mark Ahessy, who lives in Donard, a quiet village nestled deep in west Wicklow, tucked behind Blessington Lake and under Lugnaquilla Mountain at the northern end of the Glen of Imaal. There John raises his herd of full-blood Wagyu cattle, a breed that originated in Japan and is world renowned for its unusually fine marbling of high-quality fat through the meat.

Compared with other beef, the marbling in Wagyu offers more beneficial omega-3 and omega-6 fatty acids and a higher ratio of healthy monounsaturated to saturated fats, making it a healthier choice as well the most delicious one.

Wagyu cattle have a natural disposition towards this exceptional marbling. This can be further encouraged through their diet and by keeping them physically relaxed in a stress-free environment, so life in Donard suits them well. So does having their backsides massaged by a mechanical brush, which they enjoy so much that they form a (mostly) orderly queue for it.

Besides grazing on the lush summer grass that is so abundant in what's known as 'the garden of Ireland', John's herd of Wicklow Wagyu enjoy an olive feed proven to enhance the buttery flavour and marbled tenderness of the beef. No wonder Ridgeway Wagyu is a Blas na hÉireann Gold award winner.

John has also invested in a vertical strand-aligned burger machine to produce a soft-bite burger. This preserves the tenderness of his high-grade Wagyu beef without overworking the mince, which would release myosin, a protein that causes muscle contraction and a rubbery texture.

We buy Ridgeway Wagyu minced meat for our meatballs and Ridgeway Wagyu burgers, which are simply seasoned and preservative free. Then we treat that burger like a steak, cooking it on a high heat to get a nice char and let that marbling do its juicy work. As Mark puts it, 'I haven't had a better burger.'

MCLOUGHLINS BUTCHERS

Pat and Kate McLoughlin are the father-and-daughter team behind McLoughlins Butchers. Their third-generation business was established by Pat's Laois-born father, Joe, on his return from Sydney, Australia, where his work as a butcher exposed him to novel techniques and recipes. His resulting willingness to think differently in pursuit of the best results has remained at the heart of the business that Joe started in Ballyfermot in 1965.

Besides being proud to have fed generations of 'Ballyer' kids from their still-running shop, their nearby wholesale unit allowed Joe, and later Pat, to continually up their game. In particular, the dry-ageing unit that McLoughlins custom built for their beef has made them the go-to butcher for everyone from Michelin-starred chefs to food truck cooks to the most exacting of gastropub teams.

As The Old Spot general manager Denise McBrien says, 'We have been using McLoughlins beef as our staple rib-eye steak since the day we opened and our guests absolutely love it.' Indeed, Denise has been dealing with McLoughlins for years in the various fine-dining restaurants she has worked in or run and appreciates their reliably 'exceptional quality produce and service'.

Mark agrees. All good relationships are built on trust, and as head chef, he appreciates the consistency of quality, attention to detail and justified pride that he knows McLoughlins will deliver on every time. Master butcher Pat remains hands-on in the business, personally selecting the full carcasses as they come in directly from the small farm abattoir they deal with in Castledermot, South Leinster. 'They care about what they're doing,' says Mark, so he can trust that no stage in the journey from field to kitchen is compromised.

The result is tender beef with a buttery, nutty flavour and steaks that always come out top in our regular blind tastings. We also source grade-A free-range Irish chicken from McLoughlins for our Sunday roasts.

ANDARL FARM

There are pork chops, and then there are Andarl Farm free-range pork chops. The pigs are reared with care and pride by Dave and Diana Milestone and like-minded producers who they have personally vetted; the chops are cooked with care and pride at The Old Spot and served on the bone so you can relish every last bit of flavour. Once you've savoured the sweet, succulent meat that is the result of careful cross-breeding, this is a chop you'll want to pick up and get your fingers dirty for.

There's nothing else quite like it in Ireland, which is why Denise introduced Andarl to the menu at The Old Spot, having proudly served their pork at Old Street in Malahide. (A word to the wise: don't let her catch you not chewing that bone.)

Dave and Diana moved to Ireland from Yorkshire in 2010 and fell in love with a small abandoned farm near Brickens in Co. Mayo, which they named Andarl Farm. 'In England, everywhere has a name, whereas in Ireland it tends to be more based on the townland,' Diana explains. 'We decided that we should name the farm something and we couldn't come up with anything based on Diana and Dave, so we went for our pet names for each other, Angel and Darling.' And yes, she's the angel – but he's a darling.

The couple found themselves hand-rearing two orphaned piglets, Thelma and Louise, when their Great White sow mother died. These two sisters went on to become the matriarchs of the Andarl Farm herd.

Free-range rare-breed pork can be a little fatty for contemporary tastes and it can be challenging to find the perfect ratio of fat to lean meat in a free-range pig that is also hardy enough for outdoor living. After a couple of years of experimentation, the Milestones hit on their perfect cross-breed and brought Harry to the farm: a Hyroc boar cross between a Duroc and a Piétrain.

Within another few years, they were picking up top awards for their resulting pork. A prestigious Euro-toques Food Award in 2016 recognised their excellent quality standards, traditional artisan production methods and outstanding contribution to Irish food. In 2017, they became the second Irish producer to ever receive the Compassion in World Farming 'Good Pig Award' for their commitment to ethical farming practices. These husbandry standards include guaranteeing no tail docking, teeth clipping or surgical castration, and providing their pigs with appropriate bedding and the freedom to roam throughout their lives on the farm.

It's exceptional pork produced to the highest standards and we love it at The Old Spot.

SNEEM BLACK PUDDING

Mark has been eating Sneem black pudding since he was a footloose kid holidaying in the wilds of South Kerry's Iveragh Peninsula.

Quite unlike most Irish black puddings, which typically have a coarser, rustic texture, this traditional fresh blood sausage has an unusually mousse-like consistency. It's made in small-batch, tray-baked blocks and sold un-cased for slicing thick and cooking fast over a high heat to produce a crisp, crunchy exterior encasing a smooth, yielding interior with an earthy but subtle flavour.

A slice of this on toasted soda bread with Ballymaloe Relish still transports Mark back to summer mornings in caravan paradise – though he also loves to showcase its versatility in dishes like our pig's head fritter with rhubarb and pistachio or Andarl Farm pork chop with colcannon and cider jus.

Today, Mark sources Sneem black pudding direct from second-generation butcher and wool merchant Peter O'Sullivan, who is one of two Sneem butchers to produce the pudding. With the help of Michael Gleeson of Gleeson Rural Development, in 2019 Peter and neighbouring butcher Kieran Burns secured Protected Geographical Indication (PGI) status for this unique pudding. That protected status guarantees a black pudding made with sheep, cow or pig's blood, beef or lamb suet, oatmeal, onions, seasoning and spices, free from artificial colours, flavours, bulking agents and preservatives.

Each butcher makes their pudding with their own family recipes – in Peter's case, handed down from his butcher father Pete but carefully tweaked by his mother Maryann. She still keeps a close eye on things at the family's butcher shop, which Pete opened in Sneem in 1958, having trained in the trade with his uncles Mick and Denis in Cork. Peter continues to personally select all the stock that comes through their abattoir and prides himself on producing a pudding with 'a flavour not unlike the smell one gets when walking in the heather mountains and pastures where the animals graze'. He's not wrong.

WILD IRISH GAME
La Rousse Foods supply us with fully traceable, truly sustainable venison in season from Wild Irish Game. Based in Glenmalure, Co. Wicklow and working in the surrounding mountains and woodlands, they help to cull the wild herds of sika deer.

Established in 1997 and an Origin Green member since 2017, Wild Irish Game works in collaboration with national park rangers and licensed hunters, and in harmony with nature's rhythms and seasons. With no natural predators, this is deer paradise – so much so that their numbers need to be controlled in order to maintain the balance of the local ecosystem.

Higher in protein than chicken, venison is low in saturated fats and contains all 10 of the amino acids essential to human health, with twice the nutrients and minerals of beef, including high levels of B vitamins, iron, niacin and riboflavin. The meat is naturally lean thanks to the active lifestyle of these wild herds as they roam through beautiful Wicklow, past tumbling waterfalls and glacial lakes in pursuit of whatever natural vegetation they can forage (which, in the county known as the Garden of Ireland, is more than plenty).

Our chefs and our customers look forward to venison season each year and relish the chance to enjoy this natural wild game meat that is in abundant supply here in Ireland.

OUR SEAFOOD
IRISH 'GIGAS' OYSTERS
Ireland is blessed with world-class oysters thanks to our cold, clean waters, over 3,000 kilometres of coastline and deep tidal estuaries that are perfect for oyster farming due to fast-flowing tides shaping those tear-shaped shells. We serve gigas oysters (*Crassostrea gigas*), an introduced species native to the Pacific coast of Asia that now thrives around the Irish coast.

Oysters are a seasonal, regional product, so we sometimes switch up our suppliers to source the plumpest, creamiest gigas oysters year round

Sometimes we serve Harty Oysters from Dungarvan Bay, where the nutrient-rich waters of the Atlantic Ocean and the Irish Sea converge with the fresh waters running into the bay from the local rivers and streams for a unique taste with the subtlest flavour of cucumbers.

Other times we have sourced Dooncastle Oysters from the late and much-missed commercial fisherman turned oyster farmer John Ward, whose sweet oysters would start life as seedlings in Connemara and finish off in Grade A waters in Galway Bay for sweetness.

Some of our favourites come from Carlingford Oyster Company in Co. Louth, a family-run operation set up by Peter Louët Feisser in 1974 after he sailed into a misty Carlingford Lough on his hand-built wooden yacht with his wife Anna and two chickens. They never left, and today the oyster farm is run by his son Kian and daughter-in-law Mary together with the seasonal help of their two young adult children, Josh and Moya, who are studying earth and ocean sciences and marine biology, respectively. The family exports their plump, pristine oysters to some of the top restaurants in London and beyond – but happily keep lots for their Irish fans too. Their exceptional quality saw Carlingford Oyster Company win a 2024 Food Award from the Irish Food Writers' Guild.

BALFEGÓ TUNA

We source our bluefin tuna from the family-run Balfegó company built up since the 1980s by fifth-generation fishermen. They use the Japanese *ikejime* sacrifice technique to slaughter their fish in a painless and stress-free manner. This technique prevents the secretion of lactic acid into the tuna's muscles, which avoids the metallic taste this can impart to raw tuna and keeps the fish fresher for longer.

Balfegó are also market leaders in sustainable aquaculture, having invested deeply in a certified sustainable responsibility system. They catch their wild tuna in the western Mediterranean at its optimal fat point, during the early summer months of May and June, and transport it to their aqua-farming facilities near L'Ametlla de Mar in Tarragona, where it is fed exclusively on blue fish.

We believe Balfegó's bluefin tuna is second to none in terms of quality, colour, fat content and flavour. That high quality is clearly appreciated, given how much we sell at The Old Spot, where we go through about 10kg of bluefin tuna every week.

WRIGHTS OF MARINO

Wrights of Marino supply our fresh fish and shellfish, which we keep as local and Irish as possible. Our manager Denise has had a relationship with Wrights since her L'Ecrivain days and head chef Mark has been dealing with them since he started out as a chef. They both appreciate the personal touch that this family business brings to all their professional relationships.

Now run by a third generation of fishmongers, the business was established 120 years ago in 1904: first with a fishmongers and grocers shop in Malahide and then another in Marino. Over the years they developed their fish-processing skills and opened their current production unit in Howth in 1995. They now employ over 50 workers and supply hotels and restaurants around the capital city with their network of refrigerated vans, delivering fresh fish daily from their production plant in Howth.

Their fish is sourced from local fishing ports whose boats use sustainable and responsible fishing methods. They supply us with Irish mussels, clams, scallops and crab meat, Atlantic cod and sometimes even wild Irish halibut, when available.

OUR GREENS
FRUIT, VEGETABLES AND GREENS

We buy fresh fruit and vegetables from a combination of excellent suppliers.

Keelings is a third-generation family-run grower and distributor based in north county Dublin, a region of the country that has strong horticultural traditions.

Caterway is a wholesaler with family roots in the city's original Dublin Corporation fruit and vegetable market. Built in the late 19th century just behind the Four Courts off the quays of the city's Liffey River, the Victorian market was shut down by Dublin City Council in recent years with a view to redevelopment of the markets. Caterway are now based in Dublin 7.

We also love to use micro greens from Little Cress to finish various dishes for their cheerfully pretty appearance as much as their potent, concentrated flavours. Grown without chemicals in polytunnels in Ballyhack, Co. Meath by Dave Heffernan, who began his business in a garden shed that's still used for propagation, these are high-quality micro herbs and a little goes a long way. Dave's micro coriander brings a floral herb note to our Balfegó tuna, while his micro basil adds a peppery, liquorice-like lift to our arancini. Spicy red amaranth gives some peppery punch to our gnocchi and parfait, while lemon balm is useful for desserts and cod dishes.

OUR CONDIMENTS AND SPICES
REDMOND FINE FOODS

We source top-class produce from Redmond Fine Foods. Some are fresh products that bring a little luxury, such as foie gras to enrich our chicken liver parfait. Some are dry store pantry items that help us elevate dishes or elements within them: single-varietal wine vinegars; spice blends like ras el hanout for our Moroccan-spiced lamb rump and shoulder with baba ganoush; and really good-quality pistachio nuts for our chocolate and pistachio tart and skinned hazelnuts for our venison with a nut crust.

OUR DAIRY
SCÚP

Ireland has some of the best dairy products you'll ever taste thanks to the lush green grass that our herds of dairy cattle graze on for the best part of the year.

Former Wexford senior hurler Willie Devereux and his mother Siobhan decided to put that quality milk and cream to good use when they set up Scúp Gelato. Their plain creamy-textured gelato layers Madagascan vanilla flavours over a sweet lactic-flavoured dairy base, and they add only the best-quality ingredients to their small handmade batches. We love their roast banana gelato in particular and serve it with our chocolate and pistachio tart. Scúp Gelato are regular award-winners at the UK's Great Taste Awards and Ireland's Blas na hÉireann awards, and you'll understand why when you taste it.

IRISH FARMHOUSE CHEESES

Those same grass pastures and dairy herds are the basis for Ireland's wonderful farmhouse cheeses. Perhaps surprisingly, that farmhouse cheese tradition didn't really thrive in Ireland until the late 1970s, when a handful of artisan producers began to put their hearts and minds into learning all they could about cheesemaking and applying it to local supplies of Irish dairy from cows, goats and, later, sheep.

They quickly made up for lost time, and Ireland now has a world-class range of farmhouse cheeses for chefs like Mark to choose from. They also led the way for other Irish artisan producers by providing inspiration and an example of how things could be done and by helping to shape the relevant legislation to support the sector better. We have much to thank Irish cheesemakers for.

La Rousse supplies us with a selection of Irish and French cheese, which we sometimes like to change up. Nutty sheep's milk Cáis na Tíre cheese, gouda-like Coolea Cheese and fresh St Tola goat cheese have all featured on our menu. Currently we're serving an 18-month aged Comté from France and Killeen Goat and Wicklow Blue from Ireland (see page 166).

DRINKS AT THE OLD SPOT

WINE SERVICE

We take our wines seriously at The Old Spot, but not so seriously that we don't have fun with them too.

There are some exceptional producers and vintages, cuvées and chateaux represented on our wine list, and a choice of Burgundy and Bordeaux glassware to savour them in. That Château Mouton Rothschild 1981 from Pauillac, Bordeaux? That's one of many happy results of our co-owner Stephen Cooney's love of a good wine auction. It's joined on our list by several other illustrious wine names, from Vega Sicilia Unico 2009 in Ribera del Duero to Niepoort Garrafeira 1987 vintage port.

We're only getting started with our 'Irish wine geese' collection of historic Irish-related Bordeaux chateaux established by 17th-century émigrés, although we're off to a good start with a Château Talbot 2010 and Château Léoville Barton 1990, both from Saint Julien; a Château Phélan Ségur 2014 from Saint-Estèphe; and Château Lynch Bages Grand Cru Classé 1988 from Pauillac. Safe to say, if you have deep pockets, there's plenty to play with.

We also get that sometimes you just want a glass (or a bottle or two) of something delicious without digging too deep.

We are lucky here in Ireland to have an unusually broad choice of wines from all over the world, and a world-class community of small independent producer-focused importers whose passion for what they do is matched by their knowledge. We have handpicked lots of great choices from our favourite wine suppliers for every budget, with plenty of them available by the glass. We source our wine on tap from Wine Lab, which helps us cut down our carbon footprint. They also produce the excellent alcohol-free Hollow Leg wines and sparkling wines.

We also have a Eurocave wine fridge at The Old Spot, which allows us to store our wines at the optimum temperature of 16°C for red wines and 8°C for whites.

When serving wine at home, remember that some whites will be more expressive when allowed to lose their fridge-cold cool, that some reds can shine when

served a little cooler than the general rule of 'room temperature for reds', and that our interpretation of 'room temperature' has got considerably warmer over the years, so even bigger reds shouldn't be served too warm. Don't be afraid to serve richer, more full-bodied styles (think champagne and white Burgundies) at higher temperatures than simpler sparkling wines and light-bodied whites – or indeed to serve lighter, fruitier reds a little cooler than bolder, tannic reds. Twenty minutes in or out of a fridge can make all the difference: in for lighter reds, out for richer whites.

We are big believers in the value of a decanter to express a wine's full potential. We always use them for our extensive Bordeaux collection, of course, but we don't just reserve them for the top-shelf wines. Any red wines with generous tannins will benefit from the aeration that decanting offers, as will many fuller-bodied white wines. If you don't have a decanter at home, even 30 minutes in a simple glass jug will do, then you can pour the wine back into the bottle to serve.

FOOD AND DRINK PAIRING

We're a pub first and foremost at The Old Spot and are happy to serve anything from our extensive drinks list, whatever you're eating. When it comes to rules of thumb for food and drink pairing, rule number one is to drink what you like.

That said, if you'd like some inspiration as to what to drink, some solid sense can help pair food with complementary beverages. Below are some points worth considering, which can apply to beer and cocktails as well as wines.

- Pairing like with like (sweet drinks with sweet food, acidic drinks with acidic food) helps to balance out or turn down the volume on those central characteristics so that other flavours in the drinks or dishes can shine. It's counterintuitive but it works.
- Think 'like with like' to balance the intensity of flavours too and ensure neither the food nor the beverage overshadow one another. So: pair delicate flavours with one another or choose generously flavoured, full-bodied drinks to stand up to bold, robust foods.
- Matching similar aromas and flavour profiles can be a fun way to foreshadow elements of a dish, from the hard-to-beat pairing of Guinness with a beef and Guinness pie to our Sage Advice cocktail with butternut squash risotto with crispy sage.
- Consider the cooking method (roast chicken and poached chicken will shine with different drink pairings) and any garnishes and sauces that you'll be serving.
- Contrasting flavours such as sweet with salty or savoury is a classic approach for good reason. Think a proper chicken liver parfait with a serious Sauternes or blue cheese with LBV port.
- Think like a chef and play with complementary flavours. Chicken loves herbs and citrus, so pair it with a cocktail featuring grapefruit, lime and rosemary, like our low-ABV It's Sunny Somewhere.
- If pairing wine with different flavours – cheeses and chutneys, perhaps, or a buffet-style spread – consider something restrained that won't overpower the subtler flavours but with plenty of food-friendly acidity, such as Pinot Noir or northern Italian reds, or Riesling or Aligoté in whites.
- Like acidity, bubbles help cut through richness and refresh the palate, whether that's the fine mousse of a champagne or a bottle of fermented sparkling wine, the refreshing carbonation of a cold beer or the light spritz of a bubbles-topped cocktail.

At The Old Spot, we're always happy to help with drinks suggestions. We've asked bartenders Stephen and Izzy to share their recommended pairings for some of our most popular dishes throughout this book, Denise has shared some of her favourite wine pairings and writer Aoife has made a few suggestions too.

You'll also find some of our favourite food-friendly cocktail recipes at the back of this book along with pro tips and techniques from our mixology team for stocking your home bar with cocktail-friendly garnishes, purées and infusions.

We hope this encourages you to have fun with your own food and drink pairings at home. And if you have any questions, we'd be more than happy to try to answer them next time you're in with us. After all, there's probably nothing we love to talk, think and learn about more than great food and great drinks.

INGREDIENTS, MEASUREMENTS AND TECHNIQUES

OIL
For recipes that call for a neutral oil, you can use your choice of rapeseed, groundnut, vegetable or sunflower oil, each of which has a high smoke point and relatively neutral flavour.

We have specified recipes that call for olive oil. Use a good-quality extra-virgin olive oil for finishing dishes, not for cooking with.

TIMINGS
All timings are a guideline. The most important thing is to consider the end result that you wish to achieve, whether that's for the onions to be soft and translucent, the vegetables to be tender, the pastry to be golden or the meat to be falling apart.

The keys to cooking well are to pay attention and to use your common sense, but most importantly to use your senses to taste, smell, listen and look for signs of how the food is cooking.

TEMPERATURES
All oven temperatures in this cookbook are for a fan oven and are in Celsius. Increase the temperature by 20°C for conventional non-fan ovens. Remember that individual oven temperatures vary, so you may need to adjust up or down for your particular oven.

HOW TO USE A BAIN-MARIE
Some recipes call for a bain-marie, which is a way of cooking gently over indirect heat. It's useful for making custard, such as in our bread and butter pudding, for sauces like béarnaise and for gently melting chocolate.

To create a bain-marie, simply put a large heatproof mixing bowl over a pan of gently simmering water, making sure the water doesn't touch the bottom of the bowl. A metal bowl is best for conducting heat, while a plastic bowl will slow down the heating even further.

HOW TO BALLOTINE
A ballotine is essentially a sausage-shaped roll of meat (from the French *balle*, for package or bundle) that is tightly wrapped in cling film to form a compact, consistent shape. We use it for our ham hocks and other slow-cooked meat.

Besides giving a neat presentation that can then be cut into even slices before serving, this is a useful technique for storing shredded meat.

To form a ballotine, moisten the shredded meat with a splash of the cooking liquid and roll it into a cylinder. Lay out a piece of cling film on a clean surface. Put this cylinder in the centre with about 7.5cm of excess cling film on either side, then roll the meat tightly in the cling film to form a sausage shape. Tie each end tightly, checking for trapped air first. This will keep well in the fridge for four or five days or it can be wrapped in foil and popped in a ziplock freezerproof bag before freezing for up to three months.

Defrost overnight in the fridge, slice as needed and remember to remove the cling film before cooking or serving.

HOW TO BRINE

We love to use a brine to season protein like fish, white meats like chicken or pork and tougher red meats like beef cheek or oxtail. This method helps to ensure the seasoning is even and reaches all the way through rather than simply seasoning the surface layer. It also helps to firm up already meaty fish like cod, monkfish and salmon and to crisp up the skin of skin-on fillets of seabass or seabream; to tenderise cheaper cuts of red meat; and to result in moist, tender chicken with the crispiest skin.

Simply mix up a solution of 100g salt (ideally fine sea salt or pink salt) to 1 litre water and stir well until fully dissolved before submerging the protein fully. (You may wish to increase or decrease the volume of brine solution but stick with the ratio above.)

For a light brining of fish, a quick soaking of just 15 minutes is sufficient, then remove and pat dry. Some proteins such as whole chicken or pork chops will be brined overnight in the fridge, while smaller cuts such as a chicken supreme need just a couple of hours, so follow the timings given in each recipe. Generally, 'overnight' indicates at least 12 hours or up to 24 hours.

Remember that if you're refrigerating overnight, you'll need to remove the protein from the fridge and from the brine 30 minutes before cooking, pat it dry and allow it to come to room temperature.

HOW TO MAKE A CARTOUCHE

A cartouche is a closely fitting lid made of greaseproof or parchment paper that sits directly on top of food. It's useful for letting vegetables sweat in their own juices (as for our celeriac soup on page 66), for preventing a skin from forming on a sauce when holding it for any length of time (as with our pil pil sauce on page 114) and for controlling the temperature when simmering or poaching.

Ideally you should cut a cartouche to size to fit your pot or pan (you could use the pot's lid to measure) but you can use a larger piece of paper and simply tuck it down and in at the edges so it fits snugly.

HOW TO DEEP-FRY, WITH OR WITHOUT A FRYER

The key to successful deep-frying is not to overcrowd the fryer, which will reduce the heat of the oil and prevent the speedy crisping of the exterior. If necessary, work in batches.

Once you have achieved a golden exterior, finish the cooking in a preheated oven. Once the oil starts to release onto the baking tray, you will know the heat has penetrated to the centre.

If you don't have a deep-fryer, fill a large, high-sided pan no more than half-full of a neutral oil and use a cooking thermometer. If you don't have a thermometer, though, you can tell when the oil is hot enough for frying when a cube of bread dropped into the oil turns golden brown within about 40 seconds for oil heated to 150°C (or 35 seconds for 160°C, 15 seconds for 180°C or 10 seconds for 190°C).

Remember, too, that if you've cooked something fairly neutral-tasting like tostadas or chips, you can reuse the oil another couple of times to deep-fry other savoury foods. Just let it cool fully before passing through a fine mesh sieve and then rebottle. Always dispose of used oil responsibly.

HOW TO FREEZE AND DEFROST

The trick to successful freezing is to seal the food well. Ziplock freezerproof bags are useful, as is the ballotine method (see page 24) for cooked meat.

Consider how you'd like to use your food once defrosted: if you freeze concentrated, flavour-bomb liquids like our red wine jus as ice cubes, then you can easily add small quantities to other dishes while cooking. Simply pour the cooled jus into an ice cube tray to freeze, then transfer the cubes to a freezerproof ziplock bag for easy storage. Use the same technique for freezing concentrated cooking liquor from slow-braised short rib, oxtail or similar dishes.

The general rule of thumb is to freeze for up to three months. Remember to label your food clearly with a name and date and try to rotate your freezer regularly. Defrost in the fridge overnight.

HOW TO PANÉ

This is a classic method for producing a crisp breadcrumb covering that is perfect for deep-frying.

Set up three bowls: one with plain flour seasoned with a pinch of salt; one with beaten egg loosened with a little milk; and one with panko breadcrumbs. (These are a Japanese-style dried breadcrumb made from coarsely flaked white breadcrumbs that have been lightly baked to give them great crunch once deep-fried.)

Simply dust whatever you're frying (a croquette, arancini or cube of truffled mac 'n' cheese) in the seasoned flour, then dip it in the egg and finally roll it in the crumbs to cover. Set aside on a baking tray while you repeat with the rest.

HOW TO MAKE A PITHIVIER

You can serve pies family style or change things up with an individual pithivier-style pie. These work well with the chicken and chorizo or beef and Guinness pies (less so with a looser filling like the fish pie).

To make a pithivier, you will need three rolls of good-quality shop-bought puff pastry to make four pithivier along with one beaten egg, your pie filling of choice and a pinch of flaky sea salt. You'll also need two large pastry rings for this, one bigger than the other. We use a 12cm-diameter ring for the base and a 15cm-diameter ring for the top.

Before you build your pithivier, chill the filling mixture in the fridge for 30 minutes to help it set before dividing into four equal portions. Use lightly floured hands to roll the filling into four balls, then flatten the base on a lightly dusted surface. You're aiming for a shape like half a tennis ball. Alternatively, if the consistency is very loose, you could set it in a mould – a rounded coffee cup would do nicely – and freeze it for 30 minutes to shape.

Preheat the oven to 180°C.

Carefully unfold the first sheet of pastry on a lightly floured surface and stamp out four discs with your smaller ring cutter. Put one ball of the pie filling in the middle of each disc. Brush the edges with beaten egg.

Roll out the second sheet of pastry and stamp out two discs with your larger ring cutter, then repeat with the third sheet. Put these over the filling, smoothing down and out from the top to push out any trapped air. Tuck the bottom of the pastry tightly around the base of the filling, then press the edges to seal. Using the smaller pastry cutter, cut to neaten the edges and seal well all round. Brush the tops with a little beaten egg and sprinkle with flaky sea salt. With a sharp knife, pierce a hole in the centre and score lines from that centre to the edge (see the photo opposite and on page 141 for how they look pre- and post-baking). Transfer to a baking tray lined with non-stick baking paper and bake in the preheated oven for 35–40 minutes, until the tops are golden and the filling is bubbling out the edges.

HOW TO FORM A QUENELLE

'Quenelle' is the culinary term for a rugby ball-shaped oval of a semi-firm substance that can be sweet or savoury – anything from mashed potatoes or fish mousses to ice cream, sorbet or mascarpone cream.

A quenelle can be formed using two tablespoons. Warm them first in hot water, then scoop the mixture with one spoon and pass it between both spoons until you have a three-sided oval shape.

HOW TO STERILISE GLASS JARS AND BOTTLES

There are a few handy ways to sterilise your jars. One way is to simply run them through the dishwasher and leave them in the unopened dishwasher until ready to use.

Alternatively, wash them with hot soapy water and rinse well. Either put the jars on a baking tray in a preheated oven at 120°C for about 10 minutes, until fully dry, or immerse them in a large pot of cold water and bring them to a boil for 10 minutes, checking that they are fully submerged all the time.

Remember to sterilise lids and rubber seals too in boiling water for 5–10 minutes.

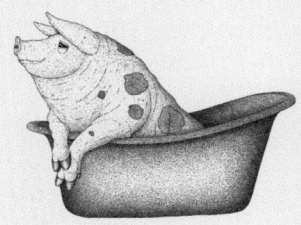

SNACKS AND STARTERS

CRAB ON TOAST

SERVES 4 AS A STARTER OR A GANG AS A SNACK

500g white crab meat, picked through twice for stray bits of shell
1 shallot, finely diced
1 garlic clove, crushed
1 fresh red chilli, finely diced
a handful of fresh parsley leaves, chopped
a handful of fresh coriander leaves, chopped
a handful of fresh chives, finely chopped, plus extra to serve
a handful of fresh basil leaves, thinly sliced
1 lemon, ideally unwaxed
a pinch of sea salt
2–3 tablespoons good-quality mayonnaise, shop bought or homemade (page 193)

TO SERVE:

4 thin slices of good-quality sourdough bread, toasted
extra-virgin olive oil, to drizzle
micro herbs (optional)
finely sliced radish
charred lemon wedge (see the chef's tip)

This can be served as a casual starter, a snack for a party or a light lunch with a crisp green salad on the side.

1. In a large mixing bowl, combine the crab meat with the shallot, garlic, chilli and herbs. Grate in the zest of the lemon, then season with salt and a squeeze of lemon juice to taste. Stir in enough mayonnaise to bind and check the seasoning again.
2. Cover and refrigerate until ready to serve (or for up to three days if you'd like to prepare it in advance).
3. To serve, toast the sourdough bread under a hot grill until crisp on either side, then drizzle with extra-virgin olive oil. Divide the crab mayonnaise among the toasts and garnish with a sprinkling of finely chopped chives, micro herbs (if using) and finely sliced radish.

CHEF'S TIP If serving this as a snack, remove the crust of the bread before toasting, then cut into even bite-size pieces after toasting and drizzling with oil. Alternatively, if serving as a starter, we like to garnish it with of a wedge of lemon that we char with a kitchen blowtorch.

DRINK PAIRING Whether you're serving this crab as an apéritif or lunch, a glass of Provençal rosé will amplify its summer vibes while tempering the kick of chilli nicely. – Aoife

LOBSTER AND PRAWN ARANCINI

SERVES 6-8

150g cooked and peeled prawns, diced (or buy raw pre-peeled Atlantic prawns and cook as outlined in step 1)
1 whole cooked lobster (see the chef's tip), meat picked and diced and shells reserved
500g cooked or leftover risotto (page 50), cooled
a generous handful of fresh basil, thinly sliced
zest of 1 lemon
100ml lobster bisque (page 197)
1 litre neutral oil, for deep-frying
300g plain flour
a pinch of sea salt
2 eggs
500g panko breadcrumbs
a splash of milk

TO SERVE:
flaky sea salt
lobster mayonnaise (page 193)
crispy basil leaves (page 206) or thinly sliced fresh basil leaves

Arancini are a Sicilian bar snack that transform leftover risotto into salty, bite-sized, deep-fried balls. They're so tasty that you might want to make the risotto especially.

1   If you're using raw pre-peeled prawns, cook them over a medium heat in a pan with a knob of butter, a squeeze of lemon and a pinch of salt for 3-4 minutes, until they lose their translucence. Allow to cool, then dice.

2   In a large mixing bowl, combine the cooked, diced prawns and the diced lobster meat with the cold risotto, then add the basil, lemon zest and just enough bisque to loosen and bind. Mix gently to incorporate, then roll into golf ball-sized balls (about 150g each) and set aside. You can refrigerate them until you're ready to cook but remove them from the fridge 20 minutes before cooking to bring back to room temperature.

3   Heat the oil in a deep-fryer to 180°C (or see page 25 if you don't have a deep-fryer). Preheat the oven to 180°C and preheat an oven tray.

4   Set up three bowls: one with the flour seasoned with a pinch of salt; one with the eggs beaten with a splash of milk; and one with the breadcrumbs. Roll each risotto ball in the seasoned flour, then dip in the beaten egg and finally coat in the breadcrumbs.

5   Working in batches, deep-fry the balls for 3-4 minutes, until golden, then transfer to the hot tray in the preheated oven for 8-10 minutes. Once the arancini start to release some oil onto the tray, you'll know they're cooked through.

6   Season with flaky sea salt and serve immediately, either with a bowl of lobster mayonnaise on the side or a dot of mayonnaise underneath, and a sprinkling of fresh basil.

CHEF'S TIP It's easier than you might think to cook a lobster at home. It will take only 8-9 minutes for a whole lobster to cook through in salted boiling water. You can keep the lobster in the freezer until you're ready to cook it, then immerse it directly into the boiling water. Or do as we do in The Old Spot and quickly drive a knife straight through into the back of head at the point where the neck joins the head.

DRINK PAIRING If you're going to the effort of serving lobster arancini and the budget allows, then surely it's champagne o'clock? Charles Heidsieck Brut Réserve is a generous food-friendly classic with opulence and elegance to match this luxurious snack. – Aoife

GIN-CURED SALMON WITH PICKLED CUCUMBER AND HORSERADISH CRÈME FRAÎCHE

SERVES 4–6 AS A STARTER OR A GANG AS A SNACK

1 side of organic Irish salmon (1–1.4kg)
50ml gin (we use Dingle Gin)
500g fine sea salt
200g caster sugar
15g fresh dill, finely chopped (reserve a few sprigs for garnish)
zest of 2 lemons

FOR THE HORSERADISH CRÈME FRAÎCHE:

200ml crème fraîche
2 tablespoons freshly grated white horseradish
1 tablespoon finely chopped chives
a squeeze of lemon
sea salt and freshly ground black pepper

TO SERVE:

Guinness brown bread (page 64)
cucumber pickle (page 205)
good Spanish capers
lemon wedges
finely sliced radish

This is a great dish as a starter or a light lunch and a lovely way to showcase the clean flavours of our excellent organic Irish salmon. It's also a handy dish for a party snack that feels luxurious but is simple to make and serve.

1. Soak the salmon in the gin for 40 minutes, turning it every 10 minutes.
2. Mix the salt, sugar, dill and lemon zest together in a large mixing bowl. Make a bed on a baking tray or in a suitably sized dish with half of this dry mixture and sit the gin-soaked salmon on top. Pour any remaining gin on top, then cover the salmon with the rest of the dry mixture.
3. Cover the tray or dish with cling film and refrigerate for 24 hours before serving (though it will keep for several more days if chilled and wrapped well).
4. To make the horseradish crème fraîche, simply mix everything together and season to taste.
5. To serve, cut the salmon crossways against the grain (not slicing horizontally, as smoked salmon is typically served, but vertically) into slices about 5mm thick. Serve four to five slices of salmon per person on sliced Guinness brown bread with pickled cucumber, good Spanish capers, a wedge of lemon and horseradish crème fraîche on the side, with some fresh dill and finely sliced radish to garnish.

CHEF'S TIP We produce excellent organic salmon in Ireland, farmed off the west coast where the fish swim against the fast Atlantic tides. It's the next best thing to wild salmon, which is exquisite but harder to source and considerably more expensive.

DRINK PAIRING A rich and rounded Chablis like our Chablis Grand Regnard would stand up to the oily salmon. – Denise

The Old Spot gives such a broad choice of Ultimate G&T serves (see page 174), all with a 50ml pour of gin. Try a Hendrick's Gin with cucumber, black pepper, pomelo and pink pepper tonic with this gin-cured salmon. – Aoife

BLUEFIN TUNA WITH AVOCADO, PONZU, SWEET AND SOUR PEPPERS AND BLACK SESAME

SERVES 4

200g black sesame seeds
200g high-quality tuna loin (we use Balfegó bluefin tuna – see page 19)

FOR THE CRISPY SHALLOTS (OPTIONAL):

2 large banana shallots
50g cornflour
a pinch of sea salt
1 litre neutral oil

FOR THE SWEET AND SOUR PEPPERS:

2 tablespoons olive oil
2 red peppers, sliced
2 shallots, thinly sliced
a pinch of saffron
100g caster sugar
200ml good-quality white wine vinegar (we use Forvm Chardonnay vinegar)

FOR THE AVOCADO PURÉE:

2 ripe avocados
1 garlic clove
juice of 1 lime
a handful of fresh coriander leaves
¼ teaspoon caster sugar
a pinch of sea salt

FOR THE PONZU DRESSING:

100ml ponzu
100ml good-quality soy sauce
30ml yuzu juice

TO GARNISH:

2 teaspoons Goatsbridge trout caviar
micro coriander leaves or roughly chopped fresh coriander leaves

This is one of our favourite starters here at The Old Spot – and it's so good, we make it twice! We give the same flavour combinations a twist with our tuna tostada, where we use tuna belly in place of the loin. It make a gorgeous party snack if you use mini tostadas. Both versions are served cold and each element can be prepared in advance, then assembled just before serving.

1. First prepare the sauces and garnishes. These can all be done in advance and refrigerated until ready to assemble and serve.
2. To make the crispy shallots (if using), peel the whole shallots, then slice them as thinly as you can to make rings – a mandolin is helpful here if you have one. Soak in iced water for 30 minutes, then drain well and pat dry on kitchen paper.
3. Combine the cornflour and salt in a shallow bowl, then toss the shallot rings in the seasoned cornflour.
4. Heat the oil in a deep-fryer to 150°C (or see page 25 if you don't have a deep-fryer).
5. Working in batches if necessary so that you don't overcrowd the fryer or pan, add the shallot rings and fry for 4–5 minutes, until crisp. Remove with a slotted spoon and transfer to a baking tray lined with kitchen paper to drain and cool. These can be made in advance and stored in an airtight container for up to five days.
6. To make the sweet and sour peppers, heat the olive oil in a heavy-based pan over a medium-low heat. Add the peppers and shallots, reduce the heat to low and cook gently for 8–10 minutes, until softened and translucent. Add the saffron and cook for another few minutes. Add the sugar and vinegar, increase the heat a little and cook until the vinegar has reduced and the peppers are sticky and glazed. Allow to cool, then cover until ready to use. This will keep well in the fridge for up to five days.
7. To make the avocado purée, blend everything together until smooth and pass through a fine mesh sieve. Season to taste, cover and refrigerate.
8. To make the ponzu dressing, simply mix the ponzu, soy sauce and yuzu together and set aside.
9. To assemble, put the black sesame seeds on a plate, then roll the tuna in them to cover completely. Lay out a piece of cling film on a clean surface, put the tuna in the centre with about 7.5cm excess of cling film on either side, then roll the seeded tuna tightly in the cling film to form a sausage shape. Tie each end tight and set aside for 30–60 minutes.
10. Use a very sharp knife to slice the tuna into four even slices before carefully removing the cling film.

11 Divide the ponzu dressing among four serving bowls, then put the tuna on top of this in the middle of each bowl. Add a small dollop or dot of avocado purée (we use a neat dot from a piping bag or squeezy bottle) and add a small twist of sweet and sour peppers. Garnish each plate with ½ teaspoon of Goatsbridge trout caviar, then with the fresh coriander, finely sliced radishes and crispy shallots (if using).

VARIATION To make Balfegó bluefin tuna tostadas, heat some neutral oil in a deep-fryer to 160°C (or see page 25 if you don't have a deep-fryer). Fry four corn tortillas (we use Blanco Niño) in the hot oil for 3–4 minutes, until golden. Remove and transfer to a baking tray lined with kitchen paper to drain and cool. These will store well in an airtight container for a few days. For the topping, use 200g tuna belly rather than the loin, chopped into small dice and seasoned to taste with togarashi, sea salt and the ponzu dressing. To assemble, put a dollop of avocado purée on top of each tostada. Spoon on a little seasoned tuna, drape over some sweet and sour peppers and dot some more avocado purée around the tuna. Sprinkle with black sesame seeds, finely sliced radish, fresh coriander and crispy shallots.

DRINK PAIRING Limeburner Pale Ale from Kinnegar in Co. Donegal is a light, crisp and refreshing beer with a touch of bitterness at the end that will pair well with the acidity of the soy and ponzu. – Stephen

The Green Door cocktail on page 177, which earned us a finalist spot in the Irish Restaurant Awards for best cocktail experience, features gin and vermouth balanced with citrus and cucumber, while ginger and pepper add a touch of spice. – Izzy

SCALLOPS WITH BRISKET, CELERIAC, PICKLED CARROT AND QUAIL EGG

SERVES 2 AS A GENEROUS STARTER

8 medium-sized scallops
200g braised beef brisket (page 82) (or the slow-braised short ribs on page 81)
100ml brisket cooking liquor
50ml chicken or beef stock (page 199)
1 teaspoon sherry vinegar
a generous knob of butter (20g)
1 lemon wedge, for squeezing

FOR THE CONFIT QUAIL EGGS:
100ml olive oil
4 quail eggs

TO SERVE:
200g celeriac purée (page 208)
pickled carrot (page 204)
a few sprigs of carrot cress or red amaranth

Perfectly seared plump scallops, gently confit quail eggs, puréed and pickled root vegetables and the crowning glory of slow-braised brisket for deep umami flavours: this is a dish to comfort while it wows.

1. Remove the coral and roe from the scallops and set the scallops aside. Discard the coral and roe.
2. Cut eight neat cubes that are each about 4cm square from the brisket and set aside any leftovers.
3. Gently heat the brisket cooking liquor with the chicken or beef stock in a saucepan. Add the sherry vinegar and adjust the seasoning to taste. Add the brisket cubes, cover and keep warm. This is the jus that you add at the end.
4. To confit the quail eggs, heat the olive oil in a small frying pan over a low heat. Crack in the quail eggs and cook them gently in the oil, being careful not to let the whites bubble and fry. Once you see the egg white starting to cook, take the pan off the heat and set it aside somewhere warm to continue cooking the eggs in the residual heat of the oil, keeping the sunny-side-up yolks nice and bright.
5. Warm the celeriac purée in a small saucepan, then transfer to a squeezy bottle or piping bag. Alternatively, cover and keep warm in the pan.
6. To cook the scallops, heat another frying pan big enough for all eight scallops over a medium-high heat. It's important not to overcrowd the pan so that you retain the heat to get a nice sear on the scallops. You can do this in batches if your pan isn't big enough and transfer the first batch to a warm plate and cover it while the second batch is cooking.
7. Add a splash of olive oil to the hot pan, then add the scallops and cook for about 2 minutes on one side for a nice golden sear. Turn them over and cook for another minute on the other side. Add a generous knob of butter and a small squeeze of lemon. Baste the scallops with the melted butter for about 30 seconds, then remove them from the pan.
8. To serve, warm four bowls. Pipe, squeeze or spoon three neat dots of celeriac purée in the base of each bowl to form a triangle. Put a scallop on top of each dot and one in the centre of the three. Nestle a cube of brisket between each of the three scallops to create a rough circle, then arrange the pickled carrots around the bowl. Spoon a little jus over the brisket, enough to give a nice thin layer in the base of the bowl without drowning the purée. Put a confit quail egg on the middle scallop and garnish with carrot cress or red amaranth.

DRINK PAIRING Consider a white wine with the acidity to cut the richness but also the body to stand up to the fleshy scallops and meaty garnish, such as the barrel-fermented Greywacke Wild Sauvignon Blanc. – Denise

DRESSED OYSTERS

We tend to leave oysters to 'the experts' to serve them to us, but they're surprisingly easy to master and such a treat to have at home. We've given step-by-step tips with everything you need to know.

WHERE TO BUY OYSTERS
You can buy Irish oysters at many good fishmongers and market stalls but also online for delivery, either direct from some producers or through those fishmongers who deliver nationwide. Most will provide an oyster knife with their oysters.

HOW TO CHOOSE OYSTERS
We serve gigas oysters (*Crassostrea gigas*), which are the most commonly farmed oysters in Ireland and are available year round. The size of the oyster can vary considerably, as do preferences. Some love them small and delicate, while some prefer them large and meaty. You can also source flat native oysters (*Ostrea edulis*) from the west coast of Ireland during the cooler months of the year. These are smaller with darker meat and are also delicious.

WHEN TO EAT OYSTERS
There was once a rule of thumb that you should only eat oysters when there's an 'r' in the month (so September through to April), which was based on two reasons: the summer months are when the oyster spawns, which is neither pleasant nor sustainable to consume; and in some parts of the world the waters get considerably warmer and more prone to toxic algae blooms during the summer. Here in Ireland, the introduced gigas oyster are farmed from seed in such a way that they don't spawn, and the cold waters and high standards for cleaning the oysters before selling them means that you can safely and sustainably indulge year round.

HOW TO STORE OYSTERS
Provided oysters have been stored cool (10°C or lower) and shipped correctly, they can safely sit in a fridge for a week. If the box is kept flat and the oysters are stacked correctly inside, they will retain their shell's seawater and maintain their perfect microclimate. Once the oyster is in good shape, its adductor muscle will hold the shell shut and keep the liquid inside. If in doubt, ask your fishmonger for guidance.

Always give the oysters a good scrub under running water before opening. As with mussels, discard any oysters that smell iffy or are open and don't shut when gently tapped on the countertop.

HOW TO SHUCK (OPEN) OYSTERS
Hold the oyster cup side down, or flat side up, using an old tea towel for grip. The towel will also soak up any seawater that might spill out while opening them and will help to protect your hand from the shell and oyster knife. The key, however, is that you shouldn't be applying enough pressure to do any damage. You want to gently slide the knife inside at or near the hinge on the pointy end of the oyster, wriggling it side to side instead of pushing it in by force. Once you feel a little give, keep shimmying it by a few centimetres and keep it horizontal. Now you can either run the inserted knife around the edge or twist the knife and pop the lid open.

Run the knife under the roof of the top shell to sever the adductor muscle and detach the meat from the shell. Remove the top lid, check the oyster and remove any stray bits of shell. Finally, run the knife under the oyster to ensure it's fully separated from the base shell and will slide off easily. For a pro touch, you can turn it over to present it plump side up.

HOW TO SERVE OYSTERS
Some people are purists and want their oysters naked or with the merest squeeze of lemon. Some are traditionalists and go no further than adding a dash of Tabasco sauce with the lemon, or swap both for a finely diced shallot in a red wine vinegar. At The Old Spot, we offer our oysters with a choice of toppings. You could choose one or two of them or go all out with all four: Bloody Mary jelly, yuzu jelly topped with Goatsbridge trout caviar, apple and mint foam and/or sake and cucumber granita (pages 212–13).

Whatever accompaniments you go for, remember that oysters are best served cold, so consider laying them out on a large tray or platter of crushed ice. Fresh clean seaweed or wild coastal vegetables like samphire can make a smart garnish and also help to keep them propped upright without spilling their juices. Alternatively, you can use a bed of coarse salt to do the same job.

DRINK PAIRING The simplest ideas are often the best, and Guinness and oysters is one of them. The saline flavours of the oyster and the light bitterness of the stout balance extremely well. – Stephen

A vibrant Rheingau Riesling like our Peter Jakob Kühn 'Jakobus' with some crystal-clear minerality freshening its orchard fruits would be a versatile match for any of our oyster toppings. – Denise

For a twist on the traditional glass of bubbly with shellfish, try a light, refreshing and zesty cocktail like our Kew Garden on page 182, featuring a cucumber and mint-infused vodka, fresh cucumber, lime juice and a splash of elderflower tonic. – Izzy

If you're going for the Bloody Mary topping, try pairing with our Bloody Mary (or Maria, with tequila) on page 184 served Old Spot-style with Buffalo sauce, green olives and a celery stick. – Aoife

PUMPKIN AND RICOTTA RAVIOLI WITH CRISPY SAGE

MAKES 6 LARGE RAVIOLI

900g pumpkin (or squash), peeled, deseeded and chopped into bite-sized chunks
3 garlic cloves, bashed
3–4 fresh sage leaves
1 sprig of fresh thyme
rapeseed oil, for drizzling
sea salt and freshly ground black pepper
150g ricotta cheese
20g walnuts, toasted and roughly chopped
a large handful of fresh parsley leaves, chopped
zest of 1 lemon
1 teaspoon PX sherry vinegar

FOR THE PASTA:

600–700g pasta dough (page 201)
1–2 tablespoons semolina, for dusting
1–2 tablespoons plain flour, for dusting
1 beaten egg, for brushing

TO SERVE:

100g squash or pumpkin purée (see page 208 for two options)
Parmesan cheese, for grating generously
1–2 tablespoons extra-virgin olive oil (use the best quality you can)
18 crispy sage leaves (page 206)

This impressive starter involves a fair bit of work but a lot can be done in advance and then assembled to serve.

1. Preheat the oven to 190°C.
2. Put the pumpkin or squash on a baking tray with the garlic, sage and thyme. Drizzle with rapeseed oil and season with salt and pepper, then toss to coat. Cover with foil and cook in the preheated oven for 45–60 minutes, until the pumpkin or squash is soft and caramelised. Remove the tray from the oven, uncover and allow to cool a little, then transfer to a large bowl. Add the ricotta, walnuts, parsley, lemon zest and vinegar and fold everything together.
3. Set a pasta machine to the thickest setting. Dust a clean work surface with semolina. Feed the pasta through the rollers three to four times on each setting until you get to the thinnest one, lightly dusting the pasta sheet with flour if required. When the pasta is as thin as you can get it, lay it out on the work surface. Cut the pasta into 12 squares (15cm x 15cm) and cover with a damp cloth so they don't dry out.
4. Spread out the 12 pasta squares. Put 1 tablespoon of the pumpkin mixture in the centre of six of the squares. Brush all around the edges with beaten egg, then put the remaining pasta sheets on top. Carefully press each one around the filling, ensuring the ravioli are well sealed and no air has been trapped. Stamp out with a large circular cutter to produce a neat round shape and refrigerate for about 15 minutes to set the filling.
5. Meanwhile, bring a large pot of salted water to a rolling simmer.
6. Using a slotted spoon, lower the chilled ravioli into the hot water and cook for about 3 minutes. (If you aren't serving them straight away, cool them rapidly in iced water and keep until later. Once out of the iced water, cut again with a smaller ring for a sharper, more exact presentation, then reheat in a pan of simmering water for 1 minute before serving.)
7. When you're ready to serve, gently warm up the squash or pumpkin purée and transfer to a squeezy bottle or piping bag. As well as being easy to control for a neat presentation, a squeezy bottle or piping bag also allows you to work quickly before the pasta can start to dry out and crack.
8. Warm four wide serving bowls and pipe or spoon some pumpkin purée into each bowl. When the ravioli are heated through, remove them from the water with a slotted spoon and gently shake off any excess water before putting on top of the purée. Add a little more purée on top, generously grate over some Parmesan cheese, drizzle with your best extra-virgin olive oil and garnish with crispy sage leaves.

VARIATION This dish works well with the slow-braised short ribs on page 81. Warm 300g cooked, shredded short ribs in 120ml of the short rib cooking liquor. Drape a spoonful over each plate of ravioli and spoon over some of the short rib juices before finishing with the cheese, oil and sage.

DRINK PAIRING A fresh, vibrant red like the wonderful amphora-aged Celler del Roure 'Safrà' from Valencia would lift this earthy ravioli. – Aoife

DEEP-FRIED TRUFFLED MAC 'N' CHEESE

SERVES 4–6

250g macaroni
30g salted butter
30g plain flour
250ml full-fat milk
250ml cream
250g Cheddar cheese, grated
75g Parmesan cheese, grated, plus extra shavings to serve
30g Dijon mustard
25ml truffle oil
sea salt and ground white pepper
neutral oil, for deep-frying

TO PANÉ:
200g plain flour seasoned with a pinch of salt
1 egg beaten with a splash of milk
200g panko breadcrumbs

TO SERVE:
truffle mayo (page 193)
fresh truffle, for shaving

TO GARNISH:
finely chopped fresh chives

This is every bit as moreish and indulgent as it sounds. Yes, we serve it as a starter. And yes, you know you want to.

1. Cook the macaroni in plenty of boiling salted water according to the packet instructions until al dente, then drain and set aside to cool.
2. Melt the butter in a large saucepan over a low heat. When the butter starts to foam, add the flour and cook for 5 minutes, stirring continuously to form a roux (paste). Add the milk and cream gradually, whisking to incorporate into the base. Continue cooking for 15 minutes to thicken into a smooth sauce, stirring to ensure it doesn't catch. Once the sauce has thickened and the flour has cooked out, add both cheeses together with the mustard and truffle oil. Season to taste.
3. Stir in the cooked pasta, then transfer to a baking dish or tray and spread it out in an even layer. Allow it to cool before covering and refrigerating for about 4 hours to set.
4. Preheat the oven to 180°C. Heat the oil in a deep-fryer to 180°C (or see page 25 if you don't have a deep-fryer).
5. Cut the mac 'n' cheese into your desired shape. Set up three bowls: one with the flour seasoned with a pinch of salt; one with the beaten egg; and one with the breadcrumbs. Dust a piece of the mac 'n' cheese in the flour, dip it in the egg and roll it in the crumbs to cover, then set aside on a baking tray. Repeat with the rest.
6. Working in batches so that you don't overcrowd the fryer, add the breaded mac 'n' cheese to the hot oil and fry for about 3 minutes, until golden, then transfer to a baking tray and cook in the preheated oven for about 5 minutes, until the oil starts to release out.
7. Serve with a dollop of truffle mayo and shave some more fresh Parmesan cheese and fresh truffle on top. Garnish with a pinch of finely chopped fresh chives.

VARIATION The truffled mac 'n' cheese makes an excellent side dish without the deep-frying. Once you've seasoned the sauce and stirred in the cooked pasta, transfer it to a baking dish, top with some more grated cheese and finish in the oven preheated to 180°C until bubbling and golden.

DRINK PAIRING Try a white Rioja like our Muga blend of Viura, Garnacha Blanca and Malvasia with the depth of flavour to amplify richness and handle robust flavours. – Izzy

BUTTERNUT SQUASH RISOTTO WITH CRISPY SAGE AND TOASTED WALNUTS

SERVES 4

100ml olive oil
2 shallots, finely chopped
300g Arborio rice
1 litre warm chicken stock (page 199)
8 tablespoons squash or pumpkin purée (page 208)
6 tablespoons grated Parmesan cheese, plus extra shavings to serve
3 tablespoons mascarpone cheese
100g cold salted butter, diced into cubes
sea salt and freshly ground black pepper

TO SERVE:
toasted walnuts
crispy sage leaves (page 206)

This method of cooking risotto allows you to par-cook the base and reserve it until you're ready to finish and serve – a handy technique if you'd like to serve a risotto for a dinner party and don't want to be standing over it, stirring away, while everyone else is having fun.

1. Heat the oil in a heavy-based pot over a medium-low heat. Add the shallots, cover the pot and sweat for 5–7 minutes without colouring, until they soften and turn translucent. Increase the heat to medium-high, add the rice and cook for another 2 minutes, stirring to toast the grains. Don't skip this important step.
2. Add 700ml of warm chicken stock one ladleful at a time, cooking it at a simmer and stirring regularly for about 8 minutes, until all the stock has been absorbed and the risotto is the consistency of a dense pudding.
3. At this stage, you can transfer the rice onto a large plate or flat tray and spread it out evenly – it's important to cool it quickly. This will keep in the fridge for a day or two. Then when you're ready to finish cooking the risotto, put the cooled risotto and the remaining 300ml of warm stock in a heavy-based pot and bring up to a simmer. Cook, stirring, for 4–5 minutes, until the stock has been absorbed and the rice is al dente.
4. Alternatively, to cook the risotto straight through without interruption, simply continue adding the stock one ladleful at a time until it has all been absorbed and the rice is al dente.
5. Stir in the squash or pumpkin purée, grated Parmesan and mascarpone until evenly combined, then remove the pot from the heat and fold through the cold butter. Season to taste.
6. To serve, divide among warm bowls and finish with some shaved Parmesan, toasted or candied walnuts and crispy sage leaves.

CHEF'S TIP Toast the walnuts at 170°C for 7–10 minutes, watching closely to prevent burning. For candied walnuts, simmer them in a sugar syrup (page 172) for 7 minutes, then dry on kitchen paper, deep-fry at 180°C for 7 minutes until golden, cool and store in a sealed jar.

VARIATION To use this recipe as a base for other flavours, either as a risotto or as arancini (page 33), simply omit the squash purée and the mascarpone while finishing it. For a vegan risotto, use vegetable stock and vegan 'cheese'.

DRINK PAIRING Our Sage Advice cocktail on page 179 has peppery spice from the rye whiskey and green bitter notes from the muddled sage balanced by juicy orange. – Stephen

OXTAIL BEIGNET WITH CARROT, ORANGE AND BLACK TRUFFLE

SERVES 6-8

700–800g brined, cooked and picked oxtail meat (page 85)
1 litre neutral oil, for deep-frying

FOR THE BEIGNET BATTER:
2 large carrots (you need 150g carrots once they're peeled, trimmed and cooked)
1 tablespoon neutral oil, plus extra for deep-frying
180ml oxtail broth (reserved from cooking the oxtail; see page 85)
2 eggs
1 teaspoon sea salt
240g plain flour
30g cornflour

TO SERVE
1 batch of orange and ginger gel (page 211)
black truffle, for grating or shaving (optional; see the intro)

Beignet can be flavoured in many different ways, so you could play around with the base recipe. We also serve these to elevate our celeriac soup on page 66. If you can't source black truffle the beignet are still delicious without it, though the truffle elevates them to something luxe.

1. Preheat the oven to 180°C.
2. Peel the carrots and trim the ends, then put them on a large sheet of foil and drizzle with the oil. Wrap them tightly in the foil and cook in the preheated oven for 1 hour. Remove the carrots from the foil and allow to cool for 5 minutes, then cut into smaller pieces.
3. Transfer 150g of the cooked carrots to a blender. Add the oxtail broth, eggs and salt and blend until completely smooth.
4. In a large mixing bowl, combine the flour and cornflour and stir in the blended carrot mixture until it's completely smooth. Keep an eye on this and stop mixing as soon as it's smooth to prevent too much gluten from forming. Transfer to a cream charger (if using) and charge the mixture with two charges, shaking well after each charge. A cream charger is a useful piece of kit for making everything from whipped cream to mousses or the lightest, crispiest beignet. If you don't have one, just whisk the batter to a light, fluffy consistency before chilling. Refrigerate overnight to set.
5. Roll 50g of the picked oxtail meat into a ball, then repeat with the rest of the meat for similar-sized balls. Refrigerate until ready to use.
6. Heat the oil in a deep-fryer to 180°C (or see page 25 if you don't have a deep-fryer). Preheat the oven to 180°C.
7. Use a ladle to shape the first beignet by filling half the ladle with batter (either sprayed from the cream charger or spooned in), placing a meatball in the centre and spraying or spooning more batter on top to cover the meat. Lower this into the hot oil and repeat with the remaining batter and meatballs, taking care not to overcrowd the oil (you may need to do this in batches). Once the beignet are golden brown, remove them from the oil and transfer to a baking tray in the preheated oven for 3 minutes. Drain on a warm plate lined with kitchen paper and season with salt.
8. Serve with a small, neat dot of orange gel on top of each beignet and a light grating or shaving of black truffle (if using – see also the variation).

VARIATION These are also delicious dressed with horseradish crème fraîche (page 34) instead of the orange gel and black truffle. You could also use slow-braised short ribs (page 81) in place of the oxtail.

DRINK PAIRING The ginger heat in our Green Door cocktail on page 177 will complement the orange and ginger gel. – Izzy

WAGYU BEEF AND FREE-RANGE PORK MEATBALLS WITH PUTTANESCA SAUCE

SERVES 4

250g Wagyu beef mince
250g free-range pork mince
50g 'nduja, chopped
a splash of olive oil
1 onion, finely chopped
2 garlic cloves, finely chopped
a small handful of fresh thyme leaves, finely chopped
100ml milk
50g panko breadcrumbs
50g grated Parmesan cheese
1 egg
4 fresh sage leaves, finely chopped
a small handful of fresh parsley leaves, finely chopped
a small handful of fresh oregano leaves, finely chopped
zest of 1 lemon
½ teaspoon smoked paprika
sea salt and freshly ground black pepper

FOR THE PUTTANESCA SAUCE:

a splash of olive oil
1 onion, diced
3 garlic cloves, crushed
1 sprig of fresh thyme, leaves picked and chopped
100g smoked bacon, chopped
6 tomatoes on the vine, roughly chopped and vine reserved
2 x 400g tins of good-quality chopped tomatoes
1 sprig of fresh rosemary
100ml chicken stock (page 199) or water
100g Kalamata olives, pitted and chopped
70g capers
a pinch of sea salt
½ teaspoon caster sugar, to taste
juice of ½ lemon, to taste
a generous handful of fresh parsley, roughly chopped

TO SERVE:

aged Parmesan cheese (we use 24-month aged), for grating
finely chopped fresh chives
sourdough or crusty bread

This is a great sharing starter in The Old Spot but you could also serve the meatballs with pasta as a main course – just double the quantity of meatballs. The secret is to use the best-quality minced meat. We use free-range pork and the incredible Wagyu beef mince (see page 16) that also features in our unbeatable burgers (page 100).

1. Preheat the oven to 180°C and preheat an oven tray.
2. Put the beef and pork mince and the 'nduja in a large mixing bowl, cover and set aside to bring to room temperature.
3. Heat a little olive oil in a large heavy-based pan over a medium-low heat. Add the onion, garlic and thyme and cook for 7–8 minutes, until soft and translucent. Remove the pan from the heat and allow to cool a little.
4. Meanwhile, gently warm the milk in a small pan. Add the breadcrumbs, remove the pan from the heat and set aside until they have absorbed all the liquid and formed a paste. Add to the mince and 'ndjua along with the cooled onion mixture, grated cheese, egg, herbs, lemon zest, smoked paprika and some salt and pepper.
5. Mix to combine, then roll the mixture into meatballs (about 150g each). Transfer to the hot oven tray and cook in the preheated oven for 25 minutes, until firm.
6. Meanwhile, make the puttanesca sauce. Heat a little olive oil in a large heavy-based pan on a medium-low heat. Add the onion, garlic and thyme and cook for 7–8 minutes, until soft and translucent.
7. Increase the heat and add the smoked bacon. Cook for a minute or two before adding the fresh tomatoes and their vine (for perfume and depth of flavour), the tinned tomatoes and the rosemary. Pour in the chicken stock or water and cook gently for 40 minutes, uncovered.
8. Add the olives and capers, then check the seasoning and adjust with salt, sugar and lemon juice to taste. Stir in the parsley and remove the tomato vine before serving. This sauce can be made in advance and will keep well in the fridge for several days.
9. To serve, transfer the cooked meatballs to a warm serving dish. Cover with the warm puttanesca sauce and finish with a generous grating of aged Parmesan and a sprinkle of finely chopped fresh chives. Serve with some charred sourdough or crusty bread on the side for mopping up the sauce.

DRINK PAIRING To balance the spice, go for a fleshy white like our Stephane Ogier Viognier or a lightly chilled fruity red like our Caruso & Minini Frappello. – Izzy

HAM CROQUETTES WITH BROWN SAUCE AND REMOULADE

SERVES 4

400g cooked and shredded ham hock meat (page 78)
100ml ham hock cooking liquid
1 tablespoon neutral oil, plus extra for deep-frying
2 large banana shallots, diced
1 garlic clove, crushed
a few sprigs of fresh thyme, picked
100g dried breadcrumbs, whizzed until fine
zest of 1 lemon
2 heaped tablespoons wholegrain mustard
a small handful of fresh parsley leaves, finely chopped
a small handful of fresh tarragon leaves, finely chopped
sea salt and freshly ground black pepper

TO PANÉ THE CROQUETTES:
2 tablespoons plain flour
1 egg, beaten
2 tablespoons panko breadcrumbs

FOR THE REMOULADE:
juice of 1 lemon
1 celeriac, peeled
approx. 6 heaped tablespoons mayonnaise (page 193 or good-quality shop-bought)
approx. 3 heaped tablespoons wholegrain mustard
a small handful of fresh tarragon leaves, finely chopped
a small handful of fresh parsley leaves, finely chopped

TO SERVE:
brown sauce (page 194 or shop-bought)
shop-bought gherkins

This dish plays with some traditional flavours that are reminiscent of home-cooked ham dinners or old-school ham sandwiches. The brown sauce cuts the fattiness of the ham, while the remoulade brings some mustard heat, celeriac crunch and the coolness of the mayonnaise to the dish.

1. Prepare, cook and pick the ham hocks as per the recipe on page 78 – this whole process will take 4–5 hours in total. Set aside 100ml of the cooking liquid to moisten the picked meat. This will help it set into croquettes thanks to the high gelatine content.
2. To make the remoulade, put half of the lemon juice in a large mixing bowl. Grate in the celeriac, tossing it in the lemon juice as you go. Add enough mayonnaise to bind it, then add mustard to taste (the measurements in the ingredients list are approximates; you may not need them all). Season with salt and pepper and add more lemon juice to taste – you want something with a bit of acidity and freshness to cut the richness of the croquettes. Cover and transfer to the fridge until ready to use. The remoulade will keep well for several days.
3. To make the croquette mixture, combine the shredded ham hocks and reserved cooking liquid in a large mixing bowl.
4. Heat the neutral oil in a heavy-based pan over a medium heat. Add the shallots, garlic and thyme, reduce the heat to low and cook for 6–7 minutes, until the shallots are soft and transparent. Add this mixture to the bowl with the shredded ham hocks and mix well to incorporate, then stir in the breadcrumbs, lemon zest, mustard and herbs.
5. To form the croquettes, press the mixture into the base of a deep rectangular dish or tray (we use a cake tin or lasagne dish) to create a dense slab. Refrigerate for at least 3 hours to set, then cut into rectangles approximately 5cm x 10cm.
6. When you're ready to cook the croquettes, set up three bowls: one with the flour seasoned with a pinch of salt; one with the beaten egg; and one with the breadcrumbs. Dust a croquette in the flour, dip it in the egg and roll it in the crumbs to cover, then set aside. Repeat with the rest.
7. Preheat the oven to 180°C. Heat the oil in a deep-fryer to 180°C (or see page 25 if you don't have a deep-fryer).
8. Working in batches so that you don't overcrowd the fryer, add the croquettes to the hot oil and fry for about 4 minutes, until golden. Transfer to a baking tray and finish cooking in the preheated oven for 4–5 minutes to heat through fully (you'll know they're done once the oil starts to release out onto the tray). Transfer to a plate lined with kitchen paper to drain.
9. Serve immediately with brown sauce and remoulade on the side and a gherkin to cut through the richness.

VARIATION For a ham hock terrine, simply add some chopped pistachios to the croquette mixture before setting, then slice (don't pané and deep-fry) and serve with an apricot purée (page 209) or plum chutney (page 210), some extra chopped pistachios and charred sourdough or brioche toast.

DRINK PAIRING The malty sweetness of an amber ale like Devil's Backbone from Kinnegar in Co. Donegal will balance the tangy brown sauce, with some refreshing hoppiness to cut the richness of this dish. – Stephen

PIG'S HEAD FRITTER WITH RHUBARB, BLACK PUDDING AND PISTACHIO

SERVES 6–8

1 pig's head, meat cooked and picked (page 88)
1 litre neutral oil, for deep-frying
200g plain flour
a pinch of sea salt
100g black pudding, cut into even dice (we use Sneem black pudding – see pages 17–18)

FOR THE FRITTER BATTER:

350g self-raising flour
2 egg whites
120ml cider
120ml sparkling water
½ teaspoon bread soda

TO SERVE:

rhubarb purée (page 210)
pickled rhubarb (page 204)
120g pistachio crumble (page 213)
finely sliced radish
baby salad leaves (optional)
micro herbs (optional)

This is traditional peasant cooking brought up to date for modern palates with all the flavour that a pig's head can offer, presented as a crispy fritter with our favourite Sneem black pudding.

1. Slow-cook the pig's head and aromatics (this will take 6–7 hours), pick the meat and set it overnight into a ballotine (see page 24).
2. Whisk all the batter ingredients together and refrigerate for at least 30 minutes or up to an hour.
3. Heat the oil in a deep-fryer to 180°C (or see page 25 if you don't have a deep-fryer). Preheat the oven to 180°C. Season the flour with a pinch of salt.
4. Slice the pig's head meat ballotine into even cylinders. Working with one at a time, roll it in the seasoned flour, then drop it into the batter, shaking off the excess. Add to the hot oil and fry for 3–4 minutes, until golden. Remove from the oil onto kitchen paper to drain, then transfer to a baking tray.
5. Meanwhile, heat a pan with a little oil over a medium heat. Add the black pudding and cook for 2 minutes on each side, then put on the tray with the pig's head fritters.
6. To serve, heat up the rhubarb purée and put a dollop on each warm serving plate. Flash the pig's head fritters and black pudding in the oven for 2 minutes, then place one of each on each plate. Add some pickled rhubarb, a sprinkling of pistachio crumble and finely sliced radishes, along with a scattering of salad leaves and micro herbs (if using).

DRINK PAIRING Kinnegar's Rustbucket Rye IPA from Co. Donegal, a refreshing IPA with spicy rye and citrussy hop notes, will cut this starter's richness while matching its earthiness. – Izzy

CHICKEN LIVER PARFAIT WITH PLUM CHUTNEY AND PICKLED CUCUMBERS

SERVES 4

300g chicken livers, soaked in milk overnight
200g foie gras, diced
1 generous teaspoon (8g) fine sea salt
a splash of neutral oil
30g shallots, diced
1 garlic clove, bashed
70ml red wine
30ml Madeira wine
100g salted butter, softened
35ml glycerine (from a pharmacy)

TO SERVE:
4 slices of brioche, toasted
cucumber pickle (page 205)
a handful of pistachios, roughly chopped
plum chutney (page 210)

This is a rather luxurious chicken liver parfait thanks to the addition of the foie gras but also the glycerine. Glycerine has very little flavour beyond a mild sweetness but it adds an amazing sheen to the finished results. We make parfait with a Pacojet, which is an expensive piece of pro kit, but have suggested how to make it at home without one too.

1. Soak the livers in a bowl of milk overnight. Don't be tempted to skip this step as it removes any bitterness that the livers may have.
2. The next day, remove the livers from the milk and pat dry. Discard the milk. Put the livers, foie gras and salt in a mixing bowl, then transfer to a vacuum-sealed bag. Place in a water bath at 50°C for 90 minutes, then increase the heat to 64°C and cook for a further 30 minutes.
3. Heat a heavy-based pan over a medium heat. Add a splash of oil, then add the shallots and garlic and cook for 5–6 minutes, until starting to soften. Add the red wine and Madeira and reduce until syrupy.
4. Transfer to a blender with the livers and foie gras, then add the softened butter and glycerine. Blend until smooth, then pass through a fine mesh sieve, pour into a Pacojet container, freeze and churn before serving. If you don't have a Pacojet you can just let it set as is, either in individual ramekins or in a tub that you 'rocher' (scoop, in chef's speak) out of later. If you use a hot ice cream scoop or melon baller, it will give a nice smooth finish to the balls.
5. Serve with toasted brioche, cucumber pickle, chopped pistachios and a dollop of plum chutney.

DRINK PAIRING For a refreshing pairing with red fruit personality, try a Plymouth sloe gin and ginger ale from our Ultimate G&T list on page 174. – Izzy

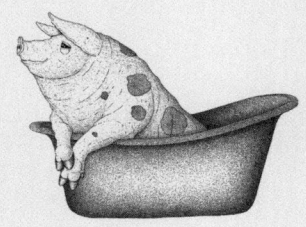

BROWN BREAD AND SOUP

GUINNESS BROWN BREAD

MAKES 1 LOAF

400g wholemeal flour
100g plain flour
35g muscovado sugar
1 level teaspoon (5g) bread soda
30g salted butter, diced and softened
330ml buttermilk
180ml Guinness stout
110g treacle
50g porridge oats

We serve this simple but delicious bread with all our soups at The Old Spot. It also makes a great base for open-face sandwiches as it's neither too dry nor too moist, but rather is nicely balanced between the two, with a slightly cake-like texture. The treacle gives it a little sweetness but is kept in check by the stout and buttermilk.

Our customers love this bread so much they buy loaves to take home, and we always have a large pre-order list for our Christmas Eve regulars.

1. Preheat the oven to 165°C. Grease a 900g (2lb) loaf tin and line with non-stick baking paper.
2. Mix all the flours, sugar and bread soda together in a large mixing bowl. Add the softened butter and rub it in with your fingertips until the mixture resembles breadcrumbs.
3. Add the buttermilk, Guinness and treacle and stir to mix through fully.
4. Pour into the prepared tin and top with a scattering of the oats. Bake in the preheated oven for 45 minutes, until an inserted skewer comes out clean.
5. Remove from the oven and allow to cool slightly in the tin before turning out onto a wire rack to cool fully.

CHEF'S TIP We like to keep this bread simple but you could also add a handful or two of pumpkin or sunflower seeds to the mixture together with the liquid ingredients, then sprinkle some extra over the top before baking.

CELERIAC SOUP WITH BLACK TRUFFLE

SERVES 4

1 tablespoon olive oil
2 medium onions, chopped
3 garlic cloves, bashed
1 sprig of fresh thyme
1 bay leaf
sea salt and ground white pepper
1.2kg celeriac, peeled and finely diced
750ml chicken stock (page 199)
200ml cream
1 lemon

TO SERVE:
1 black truffle (optional)

Celeriac has been getting more love but it's still an under-rated vegetable. Don't be put off by its gnarly appearance. Once you slice away its outer layer, you're left with a pristine root vegetable that makes a surprisingly luxurious soup.

1. Heat the oil in a large heavy-based pot over a medium heat. Add the onions, garlic, thyme, bay leaf and a pinch of salt to help release the onion's juices, cover with a lid and sweat for about 5 minutes.
2. Add the celeriac, cover with a piece of parchment or greaseproof paper pushed down at the edges to fit snugly as a cartouche (see page 25) and reduce the heat to medium-low. There is no need to cover the pan with a lid. Cook for about 15 minutes, until the celeriac is soft. Remove the paper, add the chicken stock and bring to a boil, then reduce the heat a little, add the cream and cook for a further 5 minutes.
3. Remove the thyme sprig and bay leaf before blending and passing through a fine mesh sieve. Season with salt and white pepper and a squeeze of lemon juice to taste.
4. To serve, divide among four warmed bowls and shave black truffle all over (if using).

VARIATION We like to elevate this soup even further by adding a crispy oxtail beignet (page 53) to each bowl of soup just before shaving over some truffle and serving. It transforms a humble soup into a luxe starter. Alternatively, roughly chop a handful of toasted hazelnuts and scatter these over.

DRINK PAIRING A rich white wine with some savoury character but good acidity pairs well with the celeriac and will stand up to the oxtail and truffle if you're going for the full luxe effect, maybe a rich Burgundian Chardonnay like our Viré-Clessé André Bonhomme. – Denise

HEARTY OXTAIL SOUP

SERVES 4

1.5kg oxtail
85g plain flour
a pinch of sea salt
1–2 tablespoons neutral oil
1 carrot, roughly chopped
1 onion, roughly chopped
2 bay leaves
2–3 sprigs of fresh thyme
5g black peppercorns
125g tomato purée
350ml red wine
2 litres beef stock (page 199)
100–150g pickled carrot and celeriac (page 204)

Oxtail soup is a hearty liquid lunch and a great way to use this affordable offcut. This recipe takes time rather than any great effort: a little advance planning to marinate the oxtail and patience for the slow cooking. The rewards are worth it.

1. Chop the oxtails into large manageable pieces (or ask your butcher to do this). Brine overnight (see page 25).
2. The next day, remove the oxtails from the brine and pat dry. Season the flour with a pinch of salt in a large bowl, then toss the oxtails in this to coat them.
3. Heat a large heavy-based saucepan or casserole over a medium heat. Add the oil, then the oxtails, being careful not to overcrowd the pan (do this in batches if necessary). Pan-roast the oxtails for 10–20 minutes, turning regularly and giving them your patience and attention to ensure they are evenly caramelised to a deep, dark brown colour on all sides. Set aside.
4. Add the carrot, onion, herbs and peppercorns to the pan with a little extra oil, if needed. Cook for 6–8 minutes, stirring occasionally, until caramelised.
5. Add the tomato purée and cook it out for 5 minutes, then add the red wine to deglaze the pan, stirring until the bottom of the pan comes clean. Reduce the wine by half.
6. Add the oxtails back to the pan, cover with the stock and cook gently on a low heat, uncovered, for about 6 hours, until the meat is falling off the bone. Alternatively, you could cover the pan (if it's ovenproof) or casserole with a lid and cook it in an oven preheated to 80°C for 12 hours.
7. Remove the pan from the heat. When the oxtails are cool enough to handle, transfer them from the liquid to a large bowl and shred the meat using two forks. Discard the bones and transfer the meat to a bowl. Strain the cooking liquid into another bowl and discard the solids, then cover both bowls and chill in the fridge overnight.
8. Remove and discard any fat that has solidified on top of the broth. Tip the broth into a saucepan and simmer until silky, adding more stock if the broth is too thick; it should be a soup rather than a sauce consistency. Stir through the shredded meat and pickled veg until warmed through. Season to taste.
9. To serve, ladle into warm bowls.

VARIATION Use this as the base for an oxtail ragù to serve with pasta – use the puttanesca sauce recipe on page 55 but leave out the olives and capers and stir in the braised oxtail.

DRINK PAIRING Glendalough Single Grain Madeira Cask Finish, with its sweet oak spices, will bring balance to this intensely flavoured soup. – Stephen

PEA AND HAM SOUP

SERVES 4

65g salted butter
100g smoked bacon lardons
100g shallots (4 small shallots or 2 banana shallots), chopped
1 leek, white part only, chopped
1 garlic clove, bashed
1 litre ham stock (see the intro)
1kg frozen peas
sea salt and freshly ground black pepper
80g cooked and shredded ham hock meat (page 78)

Pea and ham is a classic combination of sweet and salty flavours. This quick and easy recipe is a great way to use the leftover stock from cooking a ham hock for our croquettes on page 56, then garnishing it with a little shredded ham for texture and extra flavour.

1. Melt the butter in a heavy-based saucepan over a medium heat. When the butter starts to foam, add the bacon, shallots, leek and garlic. Cook for about 5 minutes, until the shallots are softened and turning translucent but are not coloured.
2. Add the ham stock and bring to a simmer. Add 900g of the peas (reserve the remaining 100g for a garnish by setting aside to allow them to defrost) and blend the soup immediately. Pass through a fine mesh sieve into a very cold bowl or deep tray to cool it quickly (see the chef's tip).
3. When ready to serve, combine the cooked, shredded ham hock with the reserved peas and warm gently. We do this in a small heatproof dish under a hot grill, but you could do it in a saucepan.
4. Slowly bring the soup up to a simmer, taking care not to boil it. Season with salt and pepper to taste. Divide among four warm bowls and garnish with the warm ham hock and the reserved peas.

CHEF'S TIP The keys to preserving the vibrant green colour of frozen peas in a soup or purée are to cook them for as short a period as possible and to cool them down fast by passing the peas into an ice-cold container. One handy hack is to put a mixing bowl or tray in the freezer for 30 minutes or fill it with iced, salted water to cool it right down.

DRINK PAIRING An aromatic Sauvignon Blanc with green vegetal notes would chime well with the peas, or a saline Albariño to pair with the ham, or the unique Dafni Psarades from Lyrarakis in Crete with its distinctive bay leaf notes. – Aoife

WHITE ONION SOUP WITH PICKLED GIROLLES

SERVES 4

a generous knob of butter
1kg white onions, thinly sliced
3 sprigs of fresh thyme
1 bay leaf
sea salt and ground white pepper
750ml chicken stock (page 199)
200ml cream

TO SERVE:
4 tablespoons pickled girolle mushrooms (page 205)

Onions, herbs, butter and time is a magical combination that yields a sweetness that makes this silky soup a beautiful backdrop to the earthy, piquant mushrooms.

1. Melt the butter in a heavy-based pot over a medium-low heat. When the butter starts to foam, add the onions and herbs with a pinch of salt to help release the juices. Cover with a lid, reduce the heat a little and sweat gently for 35–40 minutes without colouring, stirring occasionally to ensure the onions don't catch. Take your time with the onions, cooking them slowly and gently and making sure they don't colour. You want them to be as soft and sweet as possible, so be patient.
2. Add the chicken stock and reduce by a quarter, then add the cream and cook for another 5 minutes. Remove the thyme sprigs and bay leaf before blending until silky smooth and passing through a fine mesh sieve. Season to taste with salt and ground white pepper.
3. To serve, divide among warm bowls and add some pickled girolles on top.

VARIATION The combination of piquant mushrooms and sweet onions is a brilliant one, but if you can't get your hands on girolle mushrooms for the pickle, you could serve this soup with a garnish of mushroom duxelles instead (see page 207).

DRINK PAIRING Consider a rich New World Chardonnay made in a Burgundy style, like our wild ferment Kumeu River Chardonnay from Auckland, New Zealand. – Denise

LOW AND SLOW

THESE RECIPES FORM the basis for some of our most popular dishes here at The Old Spot. Along with making a good bone broth stock and using that to cook down a concentrated red wine, port or cider jus, slow cooking or braising is one of our favourite ways of getting a huge amount of flavour into a small bite of food. It's a magic formula for transforming humbler, tougher, fattier or gnarlier offcuts of meat on the bone – from oxtail, brisket and short ribs to lamb shoulder, ham hock and pig heads – into mouthfuls of big-hearted deliciousness.

These recipes are variations on the same core techniques, pulled together into one chapter to encourage you to master the basic approach. Some of the meats, like the beef brisket, short ribs and lamb shoulder, are seared first to add caramelised flavour (typically done in batches so as not to overcrowd the pan – if there isn't enough room for air to circulate around your meat, it will stew instead of sear). Some, like the oxtail, are brined in advance to keep them extra moist, while others, such as the ham hock and pig's head, are brought to a boil several times in fresh water to remove impurities. All are then cooked slowly and gently over a low heat with some sweet vegetables and robust herbs and spices as aromatics. Then, when the meat is fall-apart tender, we let it cool in the cooking liquor before removing and picking the meat off the bone (if there are bones), discarding any fatty or sinewy bits that would make unpleasant eating.

What we're left with is flavour gold.

The picked meat can then be used in various ways, either by adding it directly to dishes like beignet, fritters or croquettes or as the basis for hotpot and pies, ragù and even lasagne (our 36-hour slow-braised short rib lasagne is as good as it sounds). It can also be shaped into a ballotine (see page 24) for easy storage in the fridge or freezer.

Depending on the quality of the cooking liquor (and in particular the fattiness of the meat we have cooked in it), we might reduce that broth down for use in flavouring sauces.

These recipes are more time-consuming than challenging but they do require a fair bit of effort, so it's always worth making extra, either to eat in sandwiches or to freeze for another time – we've included lots of suggestions on how to store the picked meat in the fridge or freezer.

HAM HOCKS

YIELDS 900G–1KG PICKED MEAT

2 ham hocks
1 onion or 2 large shallots, quartered
2 carrots, roughly chopped
2 celery sticks, roughly chopped
1 whole garlic bulb, halved horizontally
2 bay leaves
1 sprig of fresh thyme
1 teaspoon black peppercorns

Once you master how to cook a ham hock, you can play with both the cooking aromatics and the resulting meat in different ways, giving you the basis for lots of new recipes or to add to an incredible grilled cheese sandwich.

1. Put the ham hocks in a large pot and cover with cold water. Bring to a boil until you see white scum float to the top, then strain. Repeat this process two more times, starting with fresh cold water each time.
2. Cover once more with fresh cold water and this time add the vegetables and aromatics. Bring back to a boil, then reduce the heat and simmer gently, uncovered, for 3–4 hours, until the meat is falling off the bone.
3. Strain and reserve the cooking liquor (see the chef's tip).
4. Allow the hocks to cool before picking the meat, removing any sinew or fatty bits. Two ham hocks should give you up to 1kg of meat, which can be used in various dishes.
5. The picked meat will freeze well when moistened with a splash of the cooking liquid and tightly sealed, either vac-packed or rolled into a ballotine (see page 24).

USE IN – Ham croquettes (page 56)
– Pea and ham soup (page 70)

CHEF'S TIP The cooking liquid from your ham hocks freezes well and can be used to flavour and thicken soups, stews and sauces. Consider freezing some of it as ice cubes, then pop the frozen cubes into a freezerproof bag so that the stock can be added in smaller quantities.

SLOW-BRAISED SHORT RIBS

YIELDS ABOUT 1KG PICKED MEAT

6 thick-cut meaty beef short ribs (200–250g each)
sea salt and freshly ground black pepper
1–2 tablespoons neutral oil
1 large onion, chopped
1 carrot, chopped
1 celery stick, chopped
1 whole garlic bulb, halved horizontally
150g pancetta, cut into large lardons
1 heaped tablespoon tomato purée
750ml red wine
1 litre beef stock (page 199)

A bit of time and work are involved here, so it's worth cooking more than you'll need for an individual recipe and freezing the rest for another use. We use this slow-braised short rib in lots of our dishes, including our lasagne and oxtail beignet. You could also use it with pasta or for a cottage pie to add texture to the mince, as we do in our shepherd's pie with the slow-braised lamb on page 146.

1. Season the short ribs generously. Heat the oil in a large heavy-based casserole over a high heat. Working in batches so that you don't overcrowd the pan, add the ribs and cook for 10–12 minutes, until they have taken on a rich, dark colour. Remove the short ribs from the casserole and set aside.
2. Add the chopped vegetables, halved garlic bulb, lardons and a little more oil if needed. Reduce the heat to medium-high and cook for about 10 minutes, stirring regularly, until the onions are starting to caramelise.
3. Add the tomato purée and cook for about 4 minutes, stirring to prevent it catching, then add the wine and reduce by half.
4. Add the short ribs back in and cover with the beef stock. Bring to a simmer and cook, uncovered, for 4–5 hours, until the meat is falling off the bone. Allow to cool in the cooking liquor.
5. Once cool, remove the ribs and pick the meat, discarding any fat and sinew. The cooked short rib meat will keep well in the fridge for up to five days or you can freeze it, ideally vac-packed or rolled into a ballotine (see page 24), otherwise in a well-sealed container or a freezerproof ziplock bag.
6. Strain the cooking liquor and discard the aromatics. This can be refrigerated for up to four days before using as is. Alternatively, reduce by half and freeze as ice cubes, then pop the frozen cubes into a freezerproof bag so that the stock can be added in smaller quantities to soups or stews.

USE IN – 36-hour slow-braised short rib lasagne (page 98)
– Oxtail beignet with carrot, orange and black truffle (page 53)

BEEF BRISKET

YIELDS ABOUT 900G

1–2 tablespoons neutral oil
1kg beef brisket
1 onion, roughly chopped
2 carrots, roughly chopped
2 celery sticks, roughly chopped
1 whole garlic bulb, halved horizontally
3 bay leaves
1 sprig of fresh thyme
1 star anise
500ml red wine
1 litre chicken or beef stock (page 199)

This recipe makes more than you need for the scallops starter on page 40, but it's a great excuse to cook extra and use it for sandwiches, either shredded or finely sliced, with sliced vine tomatoes, some sort of pickle, grated Cheddar, raw red onion, Dijon mustard and mayonnaise.

1. Preheat the oven to 105°C.
2. Heat the oil in a large heavy-based casserole over a high heat. Add the brisket and cook just until it gets a nice colour on each side. Remove from the casserole and set aside.
3. Add the vegetables, garlic, herbs and star anise to the casserole and cook, stirring often, over a high heat until golden brown. Add the red wine to deglaze, stirring until the bottom of the pot comes clean, then lower the heat to medium-high and continue to cook until the wine has reduced by half.
4. Add the brisket back to the casserole and cover with the stock, then bring to a simmer. Cover and transfer to the preheated oven to cook for 8 hours.
5. Remove from the oven and leave the brisket in the liquid to cool to room temperature.
6. Once cooled, remove the brisket from the liquid. Put it on a baking tray, cover with cling film or parchment paper and refrigerate for about 6 hours with some weight on top (a dish or tray with a 2-litre carton of milk sitting on top would be perfect) to compress and shape into a flat rectangle. This will keep in the fridge for up to four days.
7. Meanwhile, strain the cooking liquor and discard the solids. Store the strained liquor in the fridge for up to five days. We wouldn't recommend freezing the brisket liquor into ice cubes, like we do with some of the other cooking liquors, as it's a little too fatty for that purpose.

USE IN – Scallops with brisket, celeriac, pickled carrot and quail egg (page 40)

CHEF'S TIP You will need 100ml of the brisket cooking liquor to heat 200g of cooked brisket for the scallops starter on page 40. The remaining liquor could be used to reheat some of the remaining brisket to serve with mashed potatoes as a hearty supper.

SLOW-BRAISED OXTAIL

YIELDS ABOUT 1KG

2kg oxtail
2–3 tablespoons neutral oil
3 shallots, chopped
1 carrot, roughly chopped
1 celery stick, roughly chopped
5 garlic cloves, bashed and peeled
4 bay leaves
1 sprig of fresh thyme
200ml red wine
2 litres beef stock (page 199)
a generous splash of ponzu vinegar

As well as making the most delicious soup (page 69), we love using oxtail in a beignet, either as a standalone snack (page 53) or to bring a humble celeriac soup (page 66) to new levels.

1. Chop the oxtail into large manageable pieces (or ask your butcher to do this). Brine the oxtail overnight (see page 25).
2. Drain the liquid and let the oxtail sit for at least 30 minutes to remove as much water as possible.
3. Preheat the oven to 85°C.
4. Heat the oil in a large heavy-based casserole over a high heat. Working in batches so that you don't overcrowd the pan, add the oxtail pieces and cook for 10–12 minutes, until they have taken on a rich, dark colour. Remove the pieces from the casserole and set aside.
5. Add the vegetables, garlic and herbs to the casserole with a little more oil if needed. Reduce the heat to medium-high and cook, stirring regularly, until the veg start to colour. Deglaze the pan with the red wine, stirring until the bottom of the pot comes clean, then simmer for 2 minutes to let the wine reduce a little.
6. Add the oxtail back to the casserole and cover completely with beef stock. Bring to a boil, then reduce to a simmer and cover the top either with a cartouche (see page 25) or a lid, but not both. Transfer to the preheated oven to cook for at least 14 hours.
7. Remove the cartouche or lid and gently take the oxtail out of the broth. Allow to cool for 5 minutes, then remove the meat from the bones and fat. Stir a splash of ponzu vinegar into the picked meat to help cut the richness, then set aside to cool completely. Store in an airtight container in the fridge for up to four days or form into a ballotine (see page 24), seal well and freeze for up to three months.
8. Remove and discard the veg, garlic, herbs and any fat or gristle. Pass the cooking liquor into a clean saucepan through a fine mesh sieve and bring to a boil, then lower the heat and reduce the broth for 5–10 minutes, until it has reached a light sauce consistency with a rich, meaty, umami flavour. While the broth is reducing, use a ladle to remove any fat floating on top. Pass through a fine mesh sieve once more and allow to cool, then refrigerate until needed or for up to four days or freeze in a well-sealed container for up to three months.

USE IN – Oxtail beignet with carrot, orange and black truffle (page 53)
– Hearty oxtail soup (page 69)

SLOW-COOKED LAMB SHOULDER

YIELDS ABOUT 1.5KG, ENOUGH TO SERVE 4-6

1 x 2kg lamb shoulder
a generous pinch of sea salt
1-2 tablespoons neutral oil
2 onions, chopped
2 carrots, chopped
2 celery sticks, chopped
1 whole garlic bulb, halved horizontally
1 bay leaf
1 sprig of fresh rosemary
1 sprig of fresh thyme
1 teaspoon black peppercorns
1 tablespoon tomato purée
750ml white wine
600ml chicken stock (page 199)
600ml beef stock (page 199)

Slow-cooked lamb shoulder can become the basis for many meals, from a hearty hotpot (see the chef's tip) or pie (page 146) to a contrasting accompaniment for lamb rump served pink (page 103).

1. Trim any excess fat off the lamb shoulder and discard. Cut the shoulder into chunks (or ask your butcher to do this for you). Season with salt.
2. Heat the oil in a large heavy-based casserole over a high heat. Working in batches so that you don't overcrowd the pan, add the chunks of seasoned lamb and cook for 10-12 minutes, turning as they cook to brown all sides, until they have taken on a deep, dark, rich roast. Remove from the casserole.
3. Add all the vegetables, garlic, herbs and peppercorns to the casserole and cook for about 5 minutes, still on a high heat and stirring so the bottom doesn't catch, until nicely coloured. Stir in the tomato purée, reduce the heat a little and cook for 4-5 minutes more, stirring regularly. Add the wine to deglaze the casserole, stirring the base until it comes clean, then continue to cook until the wine has reduced by half.
4. Return the lamb to the casserole and cover with the chicken and beef stocks. Bring to a boil, reduce to a simmer and cook gently for 3-4 hours, uncovered, until the meat is meltingly tender.
5. Allow the lamb to cool slightly in the braising liquid, then use a slotted spoon to remove and transfer to a plate. Increase the heat to reduce the cooking liquor to a sauce consistency, then add the lamb back in.

USE IN – Lamb rump and shoulder with baba ganoush, tzatziki and spiced olive sauce (page 103)
– Shepherd's pie (page 146)

CHEF'S TIP This can be served as a hotpot with mashed potatoes on the side or as a lamb pie with a crispy potato topping or a pastry lid with mash on the side (see page 203). If serving as a pie, remove the meat at the end and reduce the cooking liquid to a sauce consistency, then add the meat back in and add your topping of choice.

VARIATION This can become the base for other dishes by adding different aromatics during the cooking and using the cooking liquor as a stock base for the sauce. For the lamb rump recipe on page 103, simply swap one of the onions here for a chopped leek, leave out the rosemary and thyme and add 1 tablespoon ras el hanout when cooking the vegetables, then continue as above until the lamb is cooked. Allow it to cool in the cooking liquid, then remove the lamb chunks and set aside to keep warm until ready to use. Keep the cooking liquor to use as the base for the spiced olive sauce.

PIG'S HEAD

YIELDS ENOUGH TO SERVE 6-8 AS FRITTERS OR A TERRINE

1 pig's head
2 carrots, chopped
2 onions, chopped
1 leek, chopped
1 celery stick, chopped
1 good sprig of fresh rosemary
1 good sprig of fresh thyme
1 bay leaf
20 black peppercorns
1 star anise
6 garlic cloves
1–2 tablespoons neutral oil
2 shallots, finely diced
zest of 1 lemon
1 small bunch of fresh parsley, chopped
10 fresh tarragon leaves, chopped
sea salt and freshly ground black pepper
100ml Chardonnay vinegar

This is the basis of our pig's head fritter, a relatively new dish that Mark is excited to have introduced to The Old Spot menu.

1. Put the pig's head in a large pot and cover with cold water. Bring to a boil, then drain. Repeat this process two more times, starting with fresh cold water each time.
2. Cover with cold water again and this time add the carrots, onions, leek, celery, rosemary, thyme, bay leaf, black peppercorns, star anise and four of the garlic cloves. Bring to a boil, then reduce to a simmer and cook, uncovered, for about 6 hours, until falling apart.
3. Allow to cool in the cooking liquor, then pick off all the good meat, discarding the eyes, any sinewy bits and the cooking liquor.
4. Heat the oil in a small frying pan over a medium-low heat. Finely chop the remaining two garlic cloves and add to the pan along with the shallots. Cook for a few minutes, just until softened. Add to the picked pig's head meat with the lemon zest and chopped herbs. Season with salt and pepper, then stir in the vinegar to cut through the fattiness of the meet.
5. If making the deep-fried pig's head fritters, roll the picked meat into a ballotine (see page 24) and refrigerate to set overnight or for at least 6 hours. This will keep in the fridge for up to four days or in the freezer, well sealed, for three months.

USE IN – Pig's head fritter with rhubarb, black pudding and pistachio (page 59)

VARIATION Press the picked meat into a loaf tin lined with cling film to set, then turn out to serve as a terrine, sliced into squares and served cold with crusty bread and plum chutney (page 210).

MAINS

ROAST CHICKEN SUPREME WITH GNOCCHI, SMOKED BACON, GLAZED CARROTS, PEAS AND CHICKEN JUS

SERVES 4

4 free-range chicken supremes
1–2 tablespoons neutral oil
a pinch of sea salt
20g salted butter
1 garlic clove, bashed
1 large sprig of fresh thyme
200g smoked bacon lardons
1kg gnocchi, shop-bought or homemade (page 202)
200ml chicken stock (page 199)
100ml red wine jus (page 197)
150g frozen peas, defrosted
a small handful of fresh tarragon leaves, chopped
a small handful of fresh parsley leaves, chopped
30g salted butter, chilled and diced
100g baby spinach, shredded
200g mushroom duxelles (page 207)

FOR THE GLAZED CARROTS:
4 baby carrots, leaves intact
30g salted butter
1 sprig of fresh thyme

This riff on roast chicken, peas, spuds and gravy is a perfect example of refined comfort food. While keeping that homely feel you get the freshness of the peas, the soft, spongy gnocchi and the earthiness of the mushrooms, all brought together by the buttery chicken jus. (If you love gnocchi, check out some alternative serving suggestions on page 116.)

1. Brine the chicken for 2 hours (see page 25).
2. Preheat the oven to 190°C.
3. Peel the carrots and trim the tops, leaving some green top still attached. Bring a small pot of salted water to a boil, then add the carrots and cook for about 4 minutes, until tender. Refresh in iced water and refrigerate.
4. Remove the chicken from the brine, drain well and pat dry.
5. Heat the oil in a large ovenproof frying pan over a medium-high heat. Season each chicken supreme with salt (no pepper), then add them to the pan, skin side down, and cook for 5–6 minutes, until they turn a rich, deep golden brown. Flip them over and quickly season the other side, then turn back over onto the skin side and transfer the pan to the preheated oven to cook for 7–8 minutes, until the belly-up side feels firm.
6. Remove from the oven and return the pan to a high heat. Turn the chicken over so that it's facing skin side up. Add the butter, garlic and thyme. When the butter starts to foam, use a spoon to baste the chicken skin with it for about 3 minutes, taking care not to burn the butter. Remove the chicken from the pan and allow to rest for at least 4 minutes.
7. Meanwhile, heat a small splash of oil in another pan over a medium heat, then add the bacon lardons. Once the bacon is golden, add the gnocchi and cook for 2–3 minutes on each side, until it gets a nice deep golden brown colour on both sides.
8. Stir in the chicken stock and jus. Turn up the heat and reduce the liquid for about 2 minutes, then add the peas and herbs. Lower the heat and allow to come back to a simmer.
9. Remove the pan from the heat and add the cold butter one piece at a time, stirring well to emulsify each time. Add the shredded spinach and allow to wilt.
10. In another pot, gently warm the mushroom duxelles.
11. To finish the carrots, heat a separate pan over a medium-high heat. Add the butter and allow it to melt and foam, then add the thyme and carrots. Spoon over the foaming butter to glaze.
12. To serve, divide the gnocchi, peas, bacon and sauce among warm bowls, then add a quenelle of mushroom duxelles to each bowl (see page 26 for more on the quenelle technique). Cut each chicken supreme in half lengthways and put on top with a glazed carrot.

DRINK PAIRING Marc Brédif Chenin Blanc Vouvray, with its lemon and honey flavours, would be great here, with a tangy bite to cut the richness. – Izzy

Our herb-led combination of Drumshanbo Gunpowder Irish Gin with grapefruit and rosemary tonic water (see page 174) would complement the herbaceous notes in this chicken dish. – Stephen

RIB-EYE STEAK WITH BÉARNAISE AND BEEF DRIPPING CHIPS

SERVES 4

2 tablespoons neutral oil
4 x 300g (10oz) dry-aged rib-eye beef steaks
a generous pinch of flaky sea salt
2 generous knobs of butter
6 garlic cloves, smashed
2 sprigs of fresh thyme

FOR THE SALAD DRESSING:

60ml extra-virgin olive oil
20ml Pedro Ximénez sherry vinegar (we use a 12-year-old)
1 teaspoon Dijon mustard
1 teaspoon honey

TO SERVE:

4 generous handfuls of watercress
beef dripping chips (page 120)
béarnaise (page 192)

We're proud of our steak and chips at The Old Spot, and for good reason. We source the very best rib-eye steaks from grass-fed beef that has been dry-aged by butcher Pat McLoughlin. It's a long way for our head chef Mark to come from west Wicklow on his day off, but if he's hankering for the best steak in town, he knows where to find it.

1. You can do some of the preparation ahead of time before you cook the steak and chips:
   - Prepare and blanch the chips as per the recipe on page 120, then leave them in the fridge to keep cool before cooking.
   - Remove the rib-eye from the fridge 30–40 minutes before cooking to bring it to room temperature. Pat dry with kitchen paper and season generously with flaky sea salt.
   - Whisk all the salad dressing ingredients together in a bowl or shake well in a sealed jar to emulsify. Wash and dry the watercress (but don't dress it until the last minute).
   - Prepare the béarnaise as per the recipe on page 192, cover the surface directly with cling film to prevent a skin from forming and set aside somewhere warm.

2. Once you're ready to cook the steak, heat the dripping for the chips as per the recipe on page 120. This should take about 10 minutes but keep a close eye on it.

3. Meanwhile, get a heavy-based frying pan smoking hot or as hot as you can. Add some oil and once it starts to shimmer, put one seasoned, room-temperature steak on either side of the pan to cook two at a time. Don't be tempted to overcrowd the pan, as this will reduce the heat and make it hard to get the caramelisation that you're looking for. If you have two suitable heavy-based pans, you can use them side by side; otherwise, cook the steaks in two batches.

4. Cook over a high heat for 5–7 minutes on each side to get a really rich, dark caramelisation. This will give you a medium-rare steak, which is how we recommend serving our rib-eye at The Old Spot as this allows for the flavour-carrying fat to be rendered into the meat for maximum intensity. However, if you prefer your steak done differently, see opposite for alternative timings. These are for a 300g (10oz) rib-eye, cooked from room temperature. The time duration indicates how long the steak should be cooked on each side on a high heat before turning again and basting.

Rare	(49°C–54°C)	4–5 minutes on each side
Medium-rare	(54°C–57°C)	5–7 minutes on each side
Medium	(57°C–63°C)	7–8 minutes on each side
Medium-well	(63°C–68°C)	8–9 minutes on each side

5. After turning the steak a second time (so that it's now back to the first side down), add one generous knob of butter to the pan along with three smashed garlic cloves and one sprig of fresh thyme. Once the butter starts to foam, use a spoon to baste the steaks with it for 2 minutes before removing the pan from the heat. Transfer the steaks to a warm plate and allow to rest for 4–5 minutes before serving.
6. If you're cooking the steak in two batches, hold the first batch in a warm place near the oven while the second batch is cooking, then flash the steaks in a hot pan or under a hot grill for 1 minute just before serving.
7. Meanwhile, cook the chips as per the recipe on page 120.
8. Dress the watercress leaves at the last minute.
9. To serve, plate each steak and serve with the béarnaise, watercress and chips on the side.

CHEF'S TIP The importance of resting your steak can't be overstated, as this crucial step allows the meat's muscles to relax and the juices to return into the meat. Simply transfer the steaks from the pan to a plate or tray and rest in a warm place, such as near the oven. Rest for 4–5 minutes before serving. If the steaks rest for a bit longer, you can give them a quick flash in a hot pan or under a hot grill to reheat.

DRINK PAIRING Devil's Backbone Amber Ale from Kinnegar Brewing in Co. Donegal is a full-bodied, hoppy, modern take on an Irish red ale. Those hoppy undertones bring the kind of welcome astringency that tannins in wine bring to a pairing with beef. – Stephen

Bourbon and beef is a timeless pairing, so you could keep it classy with an Old-fashioned (page 184). – Izzy

36-HOUR SLOW-BRAISED SHORT RIB LASAGNE

SERVES 4-6

2–3 tablespoons neutral oil
500g beef mince
2 onions, diced small
2 carrots, diced small
2 celery sticks, diced small
4 garlic cloves, finely chopped
2 bay leaves
1 sprig of fresh thyme
50g tomato purée
200ml red or white wine
1 x 400g tin of good-quality chopped tomatoes
250g slow-braised short ribs (page 81)
150ml chicken stock (page 199)
50g red wine jus (page 197; optional)

TO ASSEMBLE:
500ml béchamel (page 193)
200g Parmesan cheese, grated
700g fresh pasta sheets (see page 201 for homemade) or 500g dried lasagne sheets

This sensational dish tastes as good as it sounds and sells out fast whenever it makes an appearance on our specials blackboard. Yes, it takes days to make, but think of the glory! (Guaranteed.) If that doesn't seal the deal, think of the leftovers. (See the variation.)

1. Heat 2 tablespoons of oil in a large heavy-based casserole over a medium-high heat. Add the mince and brown until it's almost crispy and has turned a deep, dark, caramelised colour. Remove from the casserole with a slotted spoon and set aside.
2. Reduce the heat to medium and add another tablespoon of oil to the casserole if needed. Add the onions, carrots, celery, garlic, bay leaves and thyme and cook for about 5 minutes to soften and get a nice golden colour. Add the tomato purée and cook for about 5 minutes, then add the wine to deglaze, stirring until the bottom of the pot comes clean. Simmer for about 5 minutes, until the wine has reduced by half.
3. Return the browned mince to the casserole, then stir in the tomatoes, short ribs, stock and jus (if using). Simmer gently for about 4 hours, uncovered, stirring occasionally to ensure it doesn't catch on the bottom of the casserole. This will keep well in the fridge for up to four days and will also freeze well for up to three months.
4. Preheat the oven to 190°C.
5. Make the béchamel as per the recipe on page 193. Add the cheese and fold through until fully incorporated.
6. To assemble, cover the bottom of a large lasagne dish with an even layer of fresh or dried pasta sheets (roughly one-quarter of the pasta). Add one-third of the ragù, then one-quarter of the béchamel, then another layer of pasta. Repeat these layers two more times, then cover the last layer of pasta sheets with the remaining béchamel.
7. Bake in the preheated oven for about 40 minutes, until the top starts to turn golden and the pasta is cooked through.
8. Allow to stand for 10 minutes before cutting into slices to serve.

VARIATION Transform leftover lasagne into the most decadent snack – deep-fried 36-hour slow-braised short rib lasagne, anyone? Refrigerate the cooked lasagne overnight to set, then cut into squares or stamp out with a ring cutter. Dredge each portion in plain flour, dip into beaten egg, then coat in panko breadcrumbs and deep-fry at 180°C for 3–4 minutes, until golden. Transfer to a baking tray and cook in a hot oven at 180°C for about 5 minutes, until the oil starts to release out onto the tray. Serve with celeriac remoulade (page 56).

DRINK PAIRING Bring on the Sunday dinner vibes with a hearty red wine like our Castello di Volpaia Chianti Classico Riserva. – Izzy

THE OLD SPOT BURGER

MAKES 4

4 x 200g burgers (we use Ridgeway Wagyu or see the variation)
4 good-quality brioche buns (we use a potato-based brioche)
4 slices of Monterey Jack cheese
1 red onion, thinly sliced
4 handfuls of shredded iceberg lettuce
1 large vine-ripened beef tomato, sliced and seasoned with flaky sea salt
2 large gherkins, sliced

FOR THE BURGER SAUCE:
100ml good-quality ketchup
50ml good-quality mayonnaise, shop-bought or homemade (page 193)
30ml American yellow mustard
a splash of Worcestershire sauce
a splash of pickle juice (from the gherkin jar)
a pinch of sea salt

TO SERVE:
beef dripping chips (page 120)

We cook a mean burger at The Old Spot. Our secret? We buy in the best burgers in the land, from Ridgeway Wagyu, who raise the rare-breed beef in deep west Wicklow and make the burgers themselves (see page 16). Then we treat the burgers like a steak and cook them on a charcoal grill for extra flavour.

1. Remove the burgers from the fridge 30 minutes before cooking to bring them to room temperature.
2. To make the burger sauce, mix the ketchup, mayonnaise and mustard together and season to taste with Worcestershire for savoury depth, pickle juice for acidity and a pinch of salt to bring it all together. Refrigerate until ready to use – it will keep for up to a week.
3. Cook the burgers on a hot charcoal grill, barbecue or griddle pan for 5 minutes on each side to get a rich caramelisation. Remove from the heat, cover and allow to rest for 5 minutes. We like to serve our burgers medium-well, which is still slightly pink in the centre – use a meat thermometer to check that the thickest part of the burger is 68°C (155°F). If in any doubt, cook your burgers fully to 75°C (167°C) at the thickest part.
4. Slice the brioche buns in half horizontally and lightly toast them.
5. Put a slice of cheese on top of each burger and flash it under a hot grill for 30–60 seconds, until the cheese just begins to melt. Finish the bottom of the burgers on the charcoal grill, barbecue or griddle pan for 30–60 seconds more.
6. Spread the bottom of each bun with burger sauce, then layer up with sliced onion, a handful of shredded iceberg lettuce and seasoned tomatoes. Pop a burger on top, then add sliced gherkins, extra sauce and the top bun.
7. Serve with beef dripping chips on the side.

VARIATION You can make your own burgers using 800g of generously seasoned, good-quality beef mince. Try a mix of rump, chuck or rib-eye trimmings, maybe with some finely chopped bone marrow or smoked brisket mixed through. The keys are to keep all the fibres aligned and running in the same direction when mincing and to avoid compressing the burger when forming it or it will turn rubbery when cooked (see page 16 for more details).

DRINK PAIRING There's a reason our Muga Rioja is our best-selling red wine, especially on match days, when our burgers are in high demand. It's full-bodied with some oak spices to complement the char of our perfect burgers. – Izzy

LAMB RUMP AND SHOULDER WITH BABA GANOUSH, TZATZIKI AND SPICED OLIVE SAUCE

SERVES 4–6

1 slow-cooked lamb shoulder (page 86)
1 tablespoon neutral oil
4 x 180g lamb rumps
a pinch of sea salt
a generous knob of butter

FOR THE SMOKED ALMOND AND PARSLEY CRUST:
100g panko breadcrumbs
50g smoked almonds
50g Parmesan cheese
20g Maldon flaky sea salt
zest of 1 lemon
1 garlic clove, roughly chopped
1 bunch of fresh parsley, leaves picked

FOR THE SPICED OLIVE SAUCE:
1 tablespoon neutral oil
4 shallots, finely chopped
2 tablespoons sherry vinegar
2 teaspoons harissa
1 teaspoon honey
300ml lamb shoulder cooking liquor (page 86)
12 pitted black olives, sliced

TO SERVE:
baba ganoush (page 207)
tzatziki (page 195)

We love to bring in little bursts of flavours from around the globe and pair them with the finest Irish produce – in this case, our lamb, which is some of the best in the world.

1. You need to braise the lamb shoulder at least 4 hours before you want to serve this dish, as that's how long it will take to cook.
2. Meanwhile, you can make the baba ganoush and tzatziki in advance and refrigerate both until you're ready to serve.
3. To make the smoked almond and parsley crust, simply combine all the ingredients in a blender and blitz to a bright green crumble – just be sure the blender is completely dry first. Cover and keep dry until ready to use.
4. Once the lamb shoulder is cooked, you can use the cooking liquor to make the spiced olive sauce – you need 300ml for the sauce. Heat the oil in a saucepan over a medium-low heat. Add the shallots, cover the pan and sweat them down for about 8 minutes, until soft and translucent. Add the sherry vinegar and harissa and cook for another 5 minutes, then add the honey and lamb shoulder cooking liquor. Simmer for about 10 minutes, then pass through a fine mesh sieve and stir in the olives. Set aside.
5. Preheat the oven to 180°C.
6. To cook the rumps, heat the oil in a large frying pan over a high heat until it's very hot. Season the lamb rumps with salt, then add them to the pan and seal well, getting a dark brown colour on all sides – this will take about 6 minutes. Transfer to a roasting tray and cook in the preheated oven for 12 minutes. Remove from the oven and allow to rest for at least 6 minutes.
7. Meanwhile, heat up the baba ganoush and put it in a squeezy bottle. Reheat the spiced olive sauce.
8. Put a quenelle (see page 26) or dollop of tzatziki on four warm plates. Add a spoonful of baba ganoush and a spoonful of spiced lamb shoulder to each plate.
9. Spread out the smoked almond and parsley crust on a plate. Trim the top fat off each rump, then rub each one with a little baba ganoush and dip into the smoked almond and parsley crust, making sure to cover the top. Flash under the grill for about 20 seconds.
10. To serve, slice the lamb rumps against the grain and divide among the four plates, then drizzle with some spiced olive sauce.

DRINK PAIRING There's a lot going on here, but a powerhouse like our Mas Saint-Louis Châteauneuf-du-Pape, with its generous body and layered flavours, will be well able for it. – Denise

VENISON WITH BLACK MUSHROOM POWDER, HAZELNUT CRUST, BEETROOT, CELERIAC AND PORT JUS

SERVES 4

1 x 700–750g venison loin
1–2 tablespoons neutral oil

FOR THE BLACK MUSHROOM POWDER (OR SEE THE CHEF'S TIP):
200g wild mushrooms
15g squid ink (from good fishmongers and speciality food stores)

FOR THE HAZELNUT CRUST:
150g skinned hazelnuts
40g salted butter
20g panko breadcrumbs
½ level teaspoon (3g) fine sea salt

TO SERVE:
1 tablespoon chopped fresh chives
200g celeriac purée (page 208)
2 fresh blackberries, halved (optional)
beetroot gel (page 211)
deep-fried kale or cavolo nero (page 206; optional)
port jus (page 198)

Venison is an under-rated resource here in Ireland, but our customers love eating it as much as our chefs love cooking it. Try it at home, knowing that you are serving one of the most sustainable types of meat there is (see page 18).

1. Spread the mushrooms on a silicone sheet and drizzle with the squid ink. Put in a dehydrator at 60°C for 4–5 hours, until completely dried out. Once dry, blend to a fine powder. Keep covered and dry until ready to use.
2. Preheat the oven to 150°C.
3. Put the hazelnuts on a baking tray and toast them in the preheated oven for 15–20 minutes, watching carefully towards the end of the cooking time to make sure they don't burn. Allow to cool completely.
4. Put 75g of the roasted nuts in a blender and blitz for 45–60 seconds, just until it blends to a fine powder. Keep an eye on it and don't blend any longer than necessary as you don't want to end up with a nut butter. Add the butter, breadcrumbs and salt and blend for another 15 seconds. Transfer to a piece of thick foil and put another piece of foil on top, then roll it out using a rolling pin. Remove the top foil.
5. Finely chop the remaining toasted hazelnuts. Spread them evenly onto the crust and transfer to the freezer for at least 4 hours to set.
6. When you're ready to cook the venison, preheat the oven to 110°C.
7. Roll the venison loin in the mushroom powder to cover evenly. Heat the oil in a heavy-based frying pan over a high heat. Add the venison and cook for just a couple of seconds on all sides, working as fast as possible. Transfer the venison to a baking tray and cook in the preheated oven for 10 minutes.
8. Remove the hazelnut crust from the freezer and cut to the desired size – it should be just slightly bigger than the venison. Lay it on top of the venison and set aside to rest for 10 minutes.
9. To serve, sprinkle some chopped chives on the venison and cut into four portions. Spoon a large pool of celeriac purée on one side of each serving plate with a half a blackberry in the middle (if using). Add one or two dots of beetroot gel and some deep-fried kale for crunch and colour. Add the venison to the plate and drizzle with about 50ml port jus per plate. Serve extra jus in a jug on the side. (Any leftovers can be frozen as ice cubes to add as flavour bombs to soups and stews – see the red wine jus on page 197.)

CHEF'S TIP If you don't have a dehydrator, buy dried ceps and blitz them to a fine powder with sea salt or look for the porcini dust produced by Ballyhoura Mountain Mushrooms in Co. Cork.

DRINK PAIRING Amplify the blackberry garnish here with our Blue Blood Bramble on page 180. – Stephen

PORK CHOPS WITH COLCANNON, BLACK PUDDING, APPLE PURÉE AND CIDER JUS

SERVES 4

4 large free-range pork chops (we use Andarl Farm)
200g black pudding (we use Sneem black pudding)
1–2 tablespoons neutral oil

TO SERVE:
cider jus (page 198)
colcannon (page 203)
500g apple purée (page 209)
crispy sage leaves (page 206)

Our waiter Adrian Connor could have this dish every day of the week. It reminds him of having a pork chop for Saturday dinner throughout his childhood in the West of Ireland. There's no beating the quality of proper free-range pork and Andarl Farm produces some of the best in the land (see page 17). We pair it here with Sneem fresh blood pudding (see page 17), which has a soft, mousse-like texture, to contrast with the meaty texture of the thick-cut pork.

1. Brine the chops in the fridge for 12–24 hours (see page 25).
2. Remove the pork chops from the brine 30 minutes before cooking. Pat dry and set aside to bring them to room temperature. Cut the black pudding into four thick slices and set aside.
3. Heat the oil in a large heavy-based frying pan over a medium-high heat. Add the chops, taking care not to overcrowd the pan as that would lower the heat and you would struggle to render the fat and caramelise the meat. Use two pans or cook the chops in batches if needed, keeping the first batch warm in a low oven while cooking the second batch.
4. Render some of the fat off the edges by standing each pork chop on its side in the pan for a minute or two, then lay it flat in the pan and cook for about 5 minutes on one side until you get a rich, caramelised colour.
5. Turn each chop back on its edge to render the fat again for another minute or two, until the fat starts to crisp up and turn golden. Put it back in the pan, second side down, and cook for another 5 minutes, basting occasionally, until you get a rich, caramelised colour on that side too and a meat thermometer probe reads 68°C in the thickest part. Remove the chops from the pan and allow to rest for about 5 minutes.
6. Meanwhile, add the sliced black pudding to the pan and cook for 3–4 minutes, turning regularly to cook on all sides.
7. Flash the pork chops under a hot grill just before serving, then put each chop in the centre of a warmed plate. Drizzle over the cider jus, add a slice of black pudding on top and some colcannon and apple purée on the side. Garnish with a few crispy sage leaves.

VARIATION Serve the black pudding with apple purée on slices of Guinness brown bread (page 64) as a light lunch or hearty starter.

DRINK PAIRING With its apple and rosemary notes, our signature cocktail, The Old Spot on page 177, is a natural fit for this free-range pork. – Izzy

COD WITH ORZO, 'NDUJA, CONFIT TOMATO AND SHELLFISH

SERVES 4

4 x 170–180g pieces of cod, skinned
1–2 tablespoons neutral oil
a knob of butter
a squeeze of lemon

FOR THE ORZO:
10 confit tomatoes (page 206), halved
280g cooked orzo
1kg mussels, cleaned (see page 114)
100ml white wine
50g 'nduja (or use chorizo)
500g clams, soaked (see the chef's tip)
50g tomato passata
60ml chicken stock (page 199)
50ml prawn bisque (page 196) or an extra 60ml chicken stock
100g salted butter, chilled and diced
50g cooked brown shrimp (optional)
2 large handfuls of spinach leaves, finely sliced
a large handful of fresh parsley leaves, roughly chopped
juice of ¼ lemon
1 tablespoon sherry vinegar
1 teaspoon caster sugar

This is a beautiful way of cooking and serving cod. The brining helps to plump up the meatiness of the fish, while the final basting helps to ensure a gorgeous golden crust. The same approach works well with skin-on fillets of seabass or seabream and will result in crispy skin.

1. Brine the cod (see page 25).
2. Prepare the confit tomatoes at least 4 hours before or overnight, as per the recipe on page 206.
3. Cook the orzo in a pan of boiling salted water according to the packet instructions, until al dente. Drain and set aside.
4. To cook the mussels, heat a medium-sized saucepan until it's smoking hot. Add the cleaned mussels and the wine, cover the pan and cook for about 4 minutes, until the mussels have opened. Discard any that are still closed. Remove the pan from the heat and allow to cool, then pick the mussels out of their shells and chill in the fridge until ready to use.
5. Preheat the oven to 190°C.
6. Heat a large saucepan over a medium heat. Once it's hot, add the chunks of 'nduja. When the oil starts to render out, add the cooked orzo and the clams and stir a few times to toast in the oil, then stir in the passata and cook for 1 minute, stirring. Add the chicken stock and prawn bisque (if using) and reduce for about 2 minutes. Remove the pan from the heat and set aside.
7. To cook the cod, remove it from the brine and pat it dry. Heat the oil in a non-stick ovenproof frying pan over a medium-high heat, then put the cod in the pan, presentation side down. Cook for about 5 minutes, until the base is golden brown. Transfer the pan to the preheated oven and cook for 4–5 minutes, until only the very top of the fish remains translucent.
8. Meanwhile, to finish the orzo, return it to a medium-high heat and stir for a few minutes to reheat. Remove from the heat, add the cold butter and stir it briskly to emulsify it into the sauce (this is a culinary technique called monter au beurre that helps to add sheen and richness to a sauce).
9. Add the picked mussel meat and confit tomatoes along with the cooked brown shrimp (if using), spinach and parsley and stir over a gentle heat for another few minutes to heat through. Finish to taste with the lemon juice, a dash of sherry vinegar and sugar, if required (taste to check).
10. Remove the cod from the oven, flip it over and return the pan to a medium-high heat on the hob. Add a knob of butter and a squeeze of lemon. Allow the butter and lemon to foam up and baste your fish.
11. Take the pan off the heat and let the cod rest for a minute or two as you divide the orzo among four warm plates. Serve a piece of cod on top of each portion.

CHEF'S TIP When you buy uncooked shellfish like mussels or clams, they are still alive and should 'clam up' when handled by closing tight with their adductor muscle. Some might be a little slow to close but any that don't close when tapped gently on the counter should be discarded. See page 114 for how to clean mussels. Clams should be soaked for 30 minutes in ice-cold water before cooking. Look for the cooked brown shrimp in a good fishmonger, speciality food stores or Asian markets.

DRINK PAIRING To take a different tack, try the Cucumber Collins on page 186 from our non-alcoholic range of cocktails: a light and refreshing blend of Seedlip Garden 108, lime juice, fresh cucumber and soda. – Izzy

THE OLD SPOT

FISH 'N' CHIPS

SERVES 4

4 x 180g fish fillets (we use cod but hake, haddock or halibut also work well), seasoned generously or brined (see page 25)
1 litre neutral oil or beef dripping
200g plain flour, seasoned with sea salt

FOR THE BEER BATTER:

175g self-raising flour
½ teaspoon fast-action dried yeast
a pinch of bread soda
1 egg
125ml flavourful beer, such as an IPA or a good lager (we use Kinnegar's Scraggy Bay IPA)
a pinch of sea salt

FOR THE PEA PURÉE:

a good knob of butter
1 shallot, diced
175g frozen peas, defrosted
50ml hot chicken stock (page 199) or ham stock (page 78)
a squeeze of lemon
100g frozen peas, still frozen

TO SERVE:

beef dripping chips (page 120 – see the variation that uses oil)
tartar sauce (page 194)
lemon wedges

Great fish 'n' chips is a thing of beauty. Happily, much of the preparation can be done in advance – the pea purée and tartar sauce can be made up to three days ahead, the batter can be made and refrigerated for up to 1 hour and the chips could be prepared and stored in a bowl of cold water in the fridge overnight – making this a handy weekend dish that you could prep in the morning and finish cooking just before serving.

1. To make the beer batter, mix together the flour, yeast, bread soda and egg in a large bowl, then gradually whisk in the beer and a pinch of salt. Refrigerate the batter for at least 30 minutes or up to 1 hour.
2. Meanwhile, make the pea purée. Melt the butter in a saucepan over a medium heat. When the butter starts to foam, add the shallot, cover the pan and sweat gently for 4–5 minutes to soften. Add the defrosted peas and hot stock and bring to a boil, then immediately transfer to a blender. Blitz until smooth, then pass through a fine mesh sieve into an ice-cold bowl (see the chef's tip for the pea and ham soup on page 70). Season with lemon juice and salt to taste. Finally, stir in the frozen peas to add texture and to cool it down fast to keep the vibrant colour. Refrigerate immediately, where it will keep for several days.
3. When you're ready to cook the fish, preheat the oven to 110°C.
4. Heat the oil or beef dripping to 170°C in a deep-fryer with the basket removed (or see page 25 if you don't have a deep-fryer).
5. Set up one bowl with the flour seasoned with a pinch of salt and another bowl with the batter. Dredge one fillet in the seasoned flour, then dip it in the batter. Shake off any excess batter, then carefully lower it into the hot oil and draw it through for 4–5 seconds to allow the batter to form a protective coat before dropping the fish into the oil. Repeat with each fillet. Cook for 6–8 minutes, until golden and crisp.
6. Remove the fish with a large slotted spoon and drain on kitchen paper. To check if the fish is cooked, run a sharp knife into the thickest part of the fillet – if you feel any resistance, it might need another minute or two.
7. Sprinkle with salt and transfer to a baking tray in a low oven while you cook the chips and gently heat up the pea purée in a small saucepan.
8. Serve the fish 'n' chips and pea purée with tartar sauce on the side and a lemon wedge for squeezing over.

DRINK PAIRING Kinnegar's Scraggy Bay is a well-balanced golden IPA with a snappy bite of hops, made in Co. Donegal. – Stephen

A dry Riesling with a light spritz to lift its autumnal orchard fruit would work well with this beer-battered fish. I'm thinking of our Peter Jakob Kühn 'Jakobus', but other Rheingau Rieslings would work too. – Izzy

MUSSELS PIL PIL

SERVES 4 AS A MAIN COURSE OR 8 AS A STARTER

2kg mussels (we use Roaring Water Bay)
250ml white wine

FOR THE PIL PIL SAUCE:

2 tablespoons neutral oil
100g garlic cloves (1–2 whole bulbs), separated, bashed and peeled
80g (about 3–4) fresh red chillies, roughly sliced
50ml white wine
280ml cream
70ml red wine jus (page 197; optional)
sea salt and freshly ground black pepper

TO SERVE:

a small handful of fresh parsley leaves, chopped
1 large crusty baguette

We used to serve this as a Dublin Bay prawn pil pil, but the price of the Irish prawns rocketed so we switched to Irish mussels – a controversial move if there ever was one. Complaints were received in the strongest possible terms from regulars including Denise's sister Emma to actor Domhnall Gleeson when he turned up to dine in our front bar with some mate of his called Michael Fassbender. But there's a Team Mussels too. Many regulars agree with sous chef Naiara Passos, who says it 'combines the sweet and briny flavours of the mussel with a delicious, rich sauce with the perfect kick'. The debate rages on. Experiment at home and let us know which side you're on.

1. Wash the mussels in a colander in the sink, removing and discarding the stringy beards by pulling out and up towards the top of the shell. You can also chip off any barnacles for a cleaner presentation. Discard any mussels that are damaged or that remain open after handling. Gently tap them on the counter to check – if they don't close, discard them.
2. To make the sauce, heat 1 tablespoon of the oil in a heavy-based saucepan over a medium-high heat. Add the garlic and chillies and cook for a few minutes, until the chillies start to soften. Transfer to a blender and pulse once or twice, add another tablespoon of oil and blitz until smooth.
3. Scrape the paste back into the pan over a medium-high heat and cook for a few minutes, until the garlic smells sweet rather than pungent. Add the wine and continue to cook for another few minutes at a rolling simmer to reduce by half. Add the cream and the red wine jus (if using) and reduce by at least half to bring it to a sauce consistency. Season to taste and pass through a fine mesh sieve. You can refrigerate this sauce for up to three days before using but be sure to cover it well by placing a layer of cling film or a parchment cartouche (see page 25) directly on the surface to prevent a skin from forming.
4. Meanwhile, heat another large heavy-based saucepan over a high heat until it's smoking hot. Add the mussels and the wine, cover and cook for 3–4 minutes, until all the mussels open. Discard any that are closed.
5. Strain the mussels of their cooking stock. Stir 70ml of the mussel stock into the strained pil pil sauce, then discard the rest.
6. Pour the mussels back into the pan, then pour over the pil pil sauce and return the pan to a brisk heat for a couple of minutes to heat through.
7. To serve, divide the mussels and sauce among warm serving bowls. Garnish with chopped parsley and serve with plenty of crusty baguette. Don't forget to provide an empty bowl for mussel shells within easy reach and individual fingers bowls with warm water, a slice of lemon and a clean, crisp napkin.

DRINK PAIRING The Hop-On Session IPA from Hope Beers in Co. Dublin is a juicy, hazy, low-ABV IPA that provides the perfect hoppy bite and tropical sweetness to pair with the spicy pil pil sauce. – Stephen

Our Kool and Kurious cocktail on page 180, mixed with Hendrick's Gin, elderflower, watermelon and lime, will complement the freshness of the mussels while balancing the heat from the pil pil sauce. – Izzy

GNOCCHI WITH SQUASH, GOAT CHEESE, PINE NUTS AND CRISPY SAGE

SERVES 4

1kg gnocchi, blanched (see page 202)
a generous knob of butter
450g butternut squash, peeled and diced into 5mm cubes
1 garlic clove, crushed
1 sprig of fresh thyme
1 tablespoon olive oil
a generous handful of spinach
100g pine nuts, toasted
sea salt and freshly ground black pepper
120g crumbly goat cheese (we use St Tola)

TO SERVE:
200ml warm squash purée (page 208)
Parmesan cheese, for grating
20 crispy sage leaves (page 206)

We love cooking with squash and pumpkin, as their sweet flesh is a versatile pairing for lots of other flavours – see our ravioli on page 46 and risotto on page 50. Gnocchi is another versatile element in this dish, which can be used with other vegetables (see our cep variation) or to accompany meat or poultry, as in our chicken supreme dish on page 92.

1. Prepare and blanch the gnocchi as per the recipe on page 202. This can be done up to three days in advance. Alternatively, you can use shop-bought gnocchi and blanch as per page 202.
2. Melt the knob of butter in a large frying pan over a medium heat. When the butter starts to foam, add the diced squash with the garlic and thyme. Cook gently for 10–12 minutes, stirring regularly, until softened and golden.
3. Heat the oil in a separate large frying pan over a medium heat. Add the blanched gnocchi and cook for a few minutes on each side, until golden. Add the cooked diced squash, garlic and thyme from the other pan along with the handful of spinach. Cook to wilt the spinach, then sprinkle in the toasted pine nuts and season with salt.
4. Break up the goat cheese and crumble it into the pan. Remove from the heat immediately and remove and discard the sprig of thyme. Divide among four bowls.
5. To serve, garnish with dots of warm squash purée, season with freshly ground black pepper, grate over some Parmesan cheese and garnish with the crispy sage leaves.

VARIATION Make cep gnocchi as per page 202. Fry these lightly until golden, then add 200g wild mushrooms (we use girolles) and cook for about 3 minutes on a high heat, until they start to colour. Add 200ml chicken stock. When it starts to bubble and reduce, remove the pan from the heat, add a good knob of cold, salted butter and stir briskly to emulsify. Check the seasoning, then divide among four bowls and garnish generously with dots of garlic purée (page 209) and apricot purée (page 209) around the gnocchi. Sprinkle with four or five crispy sage leaves (page 206) per bowl and grate generously with aged Parmesan cheese.

DRINK PAIRING Our Sage Advice cocktail on page 179 has a freshness to balance the acidity of the goat cheese, while the muddled sage will foreground the crispy sage garnish. – Stephen

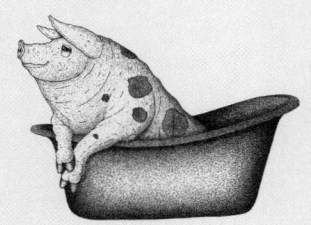

SIDES

PICKLED ONION RINGS

SERVES 4

100g caster sugar
170ml white wine vinegar
50ml water
2 large onions, peeled and cut into rings 1cm thick
500g cornflour
20g onion powder
20g garlic powder
20g smoked paprika
20g cayenne pepper
20g fine sea salt, plus extra for seasoning
1 litre neutral oil, for deep-frying

Our onion rings were always hugely popular, but this recipe introduced by Mark takes them up a notch by pickling them first. If you'd prefer to have straight-up onion rings (as Old Spot regulars Ruth and Stephen still do on their Friday night date night), simply skip the pickling step.

1. Combine the sugar, vinegar, water and 1 teaspoon of salt in a saucepan and bring to a boil, then remove from the heat. Add the sliced onions, cover with cling film and leave to cool. You can do this up to a day ahead.
2. Mix all the remaining dry ingredients together, including the 20g sea salt. Remove the onion rings from the pickling brine and shake well. Add them to the cornflour mixture, tossing to ensure they all get a proper coating.
3. Heat the oil in a deep-fryer to 180°C (or see page 25 if you don't have a deep-fryer).
4. Working in batches so that you don't overcrowd the fryer, add the onion rings and fry for about 40 seconds, until golden and crisp. Remove and drain briefly on kitchen paper, then season with salt and serve immediately.

BEEF DRIPPING CHIPS

SERVES 4

600g floury potatoes (we use Maris Pipers)
1 litre beef dripping (or neutral oil; see the intro), for deep-frying
a generous pinch of sea salt

Beef dripping adds fantastic flavour as well as crunch to these chips. If you want to cook the chips as a vegetarian side dish, you can use a neutral oil like rapeseed, groundnut, vegetable or sunflower instead, but you won't get the same depth of flavour.

1. Wash and peel the potatoes and cut into thick-cut, finger-sized chips. At this point, you can immerse them in cold water and keep them in the fridge for a few hours or overnight.
2. Blanch the chips in a large pot of boiling salted water and cook at a rolling simmer for about 3 minutes, until just tender. You only want to take the rawness out at this stage.
3. Strain well and pat dry, then spread the chips on a baking tray and allow to cool before refrigerating for at least 30 minutes, until cold.
4. Heat the dripping to 190°C in a deep-fryer (or see page 25 if you don't have a deep-fryer). This should take about 10 minutes but keep a close eye on it and check the temperature using a thermometer.
5. Put the fridge-cold chips in the fryer basket and fry for about 4 minutes, until golden and crisp. Shake off the excess oil before transferring to a large mixing bowl and seasoning with salt to taste. Serve immediately.

VARIATION To make our truffle and Parmesan chips, season the cooked chips with salt, layer with grated Parmesan cheese and truffle mayo (page 193) and finish with a generous grating of fresh black truffle all over.

CHARRED BROCCOLI WITH SMOKED ALMONDS, YUZU AND PICKLED CHILLIES

SERVES 4

500g long stem broccoli, ends trimmed
200ml Greek-style yogurt
20ml yuzu juice
a drizzle of olive oil
a generous pinch of sea salt
20g smoked almonds, roughly chopped or crushed (see the chef's tip)
20g pickled chillies (page 204)

This dish is best cooked on a barbecue with hot coals to get a deep char, but you could use a kitchen blowtorch or a very hot grill or griddle pan instead.

1. Bring a large pot of salted water to a boil. Add the broccoli and blanch for only 30 seconds, then remove with a slotted spoon and plunge directly into a bowl of iced water to refresh and stop the cooking process. Drain well and set aside.
2. Whisk the yogurt and yuzu juice together.
3. Spread out the blanched broccoli on the barbecue and cook for about 3 minutes, turning all the time to get an even char. Remove and toss in a bowl with olive oil and a generous pinch of sea salt.
4. Serve in your dish of choice (a glass dish can look dramatic), layering some of the broccoli first with a drizzling of yuzu yogurt, a sprinkling of smoked almonds and a scattering of pickled chillies. Continue to build up those layers with the remaining broccoli, yuzu yogurt, smoked almonds and pickled chillies.

CHEF'S TIP Buy the best-quality smoked almonds you can find. To crush them, pop them in a ziplock bag or inside a tea towel folded in half and bash them with a rolling pin.

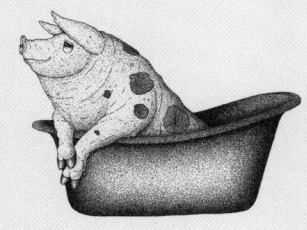

SUNDAY ROASTS

Our Sunday roasts are legendary. Word has spread beyond our immediate neighbourhood, where they are a local institution. People are known to regularly travel across the city for our dream of a roast dinner, served with all the trimmings and sides you'd hope for.

Dublin native Colin Farrell often makes a special Sunday trip for the roast chicken and all the trimmings, while his vegetarian brother and Old Spot regular Eamonn Farrell makes regular trips just for the trimmings, which make a meal in themselves. Our roast chicken is the highlight of bartender Izzy's working week, as it reminds her of her childhood; she looks forward to having it every Sunday for our staff meal. Our food runner Conor O'Buachalla describes our roast beef as 'the nicest beef and gravy I've ever had, with lovely crispy roasties. Everything on the plate is full of flavour. It's the perfect roast for me.'

WHAT MAKES OUR ROAST DINNERS SO SPECIAL?
We keep things relatively simple and we focus on delivering the very best version of every element. We source the best meat, for a start. Free-range Irish chicken that has had the freedom to roam and build up flavour in those thighs and wings for a well-developed bird. Tender, flavoursome cuts of grass-fed Irish beef from one of the best butchers we know, who gives his dry-aged beef the long hanging time it deserves.

Then we handle that meat carefully, respectfully and patiently to get the best we can out of it. We always brine our chicken overnight to season the bird evenly all the way through and also to ensure moist, tender meat and the crispiest skin. We slow-roast our beef overnight to allow the fibres to relax and break down slowly, which lets that flavour and texture sing.

And we serve these show-stopper centrepieces with the finest gravy, stuffing and sides. Duck fat roasties for the crispiest of crunches. Sweet roast carrots and creamy cauliflower cheese. Nutty, fruity, herby stuffing and fluffy Yorkshire puddings for mopping up that rich, savoury gravy.

We make it look easy, but a fair bit of work goes into mastering the perfect Sunday roast. If you'd like to master it too, there are a few key points to consider.

- Timing and oven temperatures are key in terms of co-ordinating the various elements of your roast. Remember that your centrepiece bird or cut of beef will require the longest time in the oven but also that you'll be allowing it to rest before serving, which gives you time to finish the various sides.
- You can do much of the work in advance or while your meat is roasting. Our Sunday roast gravy, for example, incorporates the roasting juices into the finished result but the base could be started the day before. The Yorkshire pudding batter can be made the day before or that morning, while the carrots and the cauliflower can be blanched ahead of time and the potatoes can be peeled and prepped in advance too.
- We slow-roast our beef at too low a temperature for sides like roasties and Yorkshire puddings but resting it for at least 30 minutes gives you time to crank up the oven to 180°C to finish cooking all the trimmings. Likewise, we like to cook our chicken in a hot oven, but once the bird is cooked you can lower the heat to 180°C to complete the other elements.

When planning your timings, bear a few things in mind.

- You can hold your meat for longer than the minimum resting time, along with any side dishes that are ready, by keeping them in a low oven (if you have a second oven) or by wrapping them in foil and then covering them with a tea towel to retain the heat, then unwrapping and flashing them in the hot oven or under a hot grill for a couple of minutes before serving.
- Try to co-ordinate the sides so that everything is more or less ready at the same time but remember that you can happily hold them for 5–10 minutes while something else finishes cooking.
- If you're cooking Yorkshire puddings, you'll need to plan the timings extra carefully so that you're not opening the oven door while the puddings are rising at the start. For example, give your roast potatoes a 5-minute head start before adding the Yorkshire puddings, stuffing, carrots and cauliflower cheese to the oven. You can turn the spuds and check the carrots when you're taking out the stuffing after 25 minutes, then turn the spuds again and check the Yorkshire puddings when you're taking out the cauliflower.

Don't forget to open that nice bottle of wine and let it breathe at the right temperature (see pages 22–23 for suggested serving temperatures and advice on decanting). After all, it's not Sunday every day of the week.

ROAST CHICKEN DINNER

SERVES 4

1 x 1.5–1.8kg free-range or organic chicken (see the chef's tip)
1 onion, roughly chopped in large chunks
1 carrot, roughly chopped in large chunks
1 celery stick, roughly chopped in large chunks
4 garlic cloves, bashed
1 sprig of fresh thyme
a drizzle of olive oil
1 lemon
a pinch of sea salt

TO SERVE:
Sunday roast gravy (page 200)

Our roast chicken dinner is the talk of the town. People will – and do – travel for it. The trick is good sourcing of the bird itself, overnight brining to ensure the juiciest meat and the crispest skin, then attention to detail for all the trimmings.

1. Brine the chicken in the fridge overnight (see page 25).
2. At least 30–40 minutes before cooking, remove the chicken from the brine, pat it dry and allow it to come to room temperature.
3. Preheat the oven to 240°C.
4. Put the vegetables, garlic and thyme in a baking tray and drizzle with olive oil, tossing to coat. Pierce the whole lemon with the tip of a sharp knife a few times and put it inside the bird's cavity. Season the chicken generously with salt and rub olive oil all over it. Put the chicken on top of the vegetables and transfer the tray to the oven.
5. Reduce the heat to 200°C and cook for about 80 minutes, until the thickest part of the thigh reaches 75°C (use a meat thermometer to check) or the juices run clear when you skewer the thickest part of the thigh.
6. Remove the tray from the oven, transfer the chicken to a large plate or board, cover with foil and allow to rest for at least 20 minutes.
7. Meanwhile, make the gravy and finish the side dishes.
8. To carve the chicken, use a sharp knife to remove the wishbone first and separate the legs and thighs from the carcass. Remove the whole breast, taking the whole thing off intact, then turn it upside down on a board before slicing, which helps keep the skin nice and neat.

CHEF'S TIP Always go for a local, free-range or organic chicken if you can. The resulting texture and flavour are better, plus you know where it's coming from and are supporting local producers. Get the most value out of any leftovers by using them in our chicken and chorizo pie (page 140).

DRINK PAIRING Picollo Ernesto's Gavi di Gavi 'Rovereto' from Piedmont has been on all my wine lists since 2009. It's a brilliant example of just how refreshing a good Gavi di Gavi can be, with crisp lemon character, refreshing minerality and hints of almond. – Denise

If you'd like to keep things refreshing, It's Sunny Somewhere on page 182 is a citrussy cocktail with a hint of tartness to make you keep coming back for more. – Stephen

SUNDAY ROAST BEEF

SERVES 4

1 tablespoon neutral oil
800g–1kg beef rump (see the intro)
a pinch of sea salt
1 onion, roughly chopped
1 carrot, roughly chopped
1 celery stick, roughly chopped
1 whole garlic bulb, halved horizontally
1 small bunch of fresh thyme
Sunday roast gravy (page 200), to serve

Roast rump of beef hits that sweet spot between value, flavour and texture. It has a little chew to it but our slow-roast method keeps it tender. Most importantly, it has incredible flavour. Use the best butcher and the best grass-fed beef you can buy for your roast and ask for rump heart, the most tender of the three rump muscles.

1. Preheat the oven to 55°C.
2. Heat a heavy-based frying pan over a high heat. When it's hot, add the oil. Season the beef all over with salt, then put it in the pan and cook, turning regularly, until you get a dark, rich caramelisation all over.
3. In a roasting tray, toss the vegetables, garlic and thyme in a little oil, then sit the beef on top of them like a trivet.
4. Cook in the preheated oven for 5–6 hours, until the internal temperature in the centre of the beef hits 55°C (use a meat thermometer probe to check). There is no need to baste the meat while it cooks with this slow-roasting method.
5. Transfer the beef to a large plate or board, cover with foil and allow to rest in a warm place for at least 30 minutes before carving and serving.
6. Meanwhile, finish the side dishes while the beef is resting. Finish the gravy by incorporating the meat juices from the roasting tray and squeezing in the roast garlic from the halved bulb too.
7. If you want to rest the beef for longer, you can flash it in a hot oven or under a very hot grill for a minute before serving. Be sure to serve on hot plates and with hot gravy too.

CHEF'S TIP The above timings and temperature are for medium-rare beef. Set the oven to 60°C for medium-well or 70°C for well done.

VARIATION For a blow-out treat, roast rib of beef can be cooked using the same technique and timings as the rump.

DRINK PAIRING Another favourite wine that has been on all my wine lists since 2009 is La Casetta Valpolicella Ripasso, a velvety treat of an Italian red with both polish and comfort. – Denise

If your Sunday roast is a Sunday lunch after the night before, our Bloody Mary on page 184 is the ultimate hangover cure. Served with a cool celery stalk and green olives to balance the spice from the Tabasco and Buffalo sauce, it's an indulgent treat with the roast beef. – Izzy

ROAST CARROTS

SERVES 4

1 bunch of carrots (about 6–8), tops intact
1–2 tablespoons olive oil
3 garlic cloves, bashed
1 sprig of fresh thyme
5 black peppercorns
1 star anise
a pinch of sea salt
1 tablespoon red wine vinegar
1 tablespoon maple syrup

The trick here is to use the best, freshest carrots you can find – look for a bunch of carrots with the tops still intact.

1. Preheat the oven to 180°C. Put a baking tray in the oven while it preheats.
2. Cut the tops off the carrots (see the chef's tip for how to use these), leaving just a little green still attached. Scrub the carrots well.
3. Bring a large pot of salted water to a boil. Add the whole carrots and blanch for about 4 minutes, until just tender. Remove the carrots from the water and pat dry.
4. Heat the oil in a frying pan over a medium-high heat. Add the garlic, thyme, peppercorns and star anise and cook for 1–2 minutes, until fragrant. Add the blanched carrots, season with salt and pan-roast just until they are starting to take on some colour.
5. Transfer to the heated baking tray, add the vinegar and maple syrup, cover with foil and roast in the preheated oven for 25–30 minutes, until tender. Discard the aromatics before serving.

CHEF'S TIP Fresh carrot tops are edible and full of vitamins. They taste like mild parsley and work well as a base for a pesto combined with your choice of other herbs and leaves like spinach, rocket, wild garlic or coriander.

SAGE, APRICOT AND WALNUT STUFFING

SERVES 4, WITH LEFTOVERS

100g salted butter
2 small onions, finely chopped
2 garlic cloves, chopped
1 sprig of fresh thyme
250ml chicken stock (page 199)
600g fresh breadcrumbs
200g dried apricots, roughly chopped
200g walnuts, roughly chopped
1 small bunch of fresh parsley, roughly chopped
zest of 1 lemon
½ teaspoon finely chopped fresh sage
½ teaspoon garlic powder
½ teaspoon onion powder
½ teaspoon fine sea salt
½ teaspoon freshly ground black pepper

Stuffing is essential. This is a generous recipe that will ensure leftovers for tomorrow's sandwiches.

1. Preheat the oven to 180°C.
2. Melt the butter in a large saucepan over a medium-low heat. When the butter starts to foam, add the onions, garlic and thyme. Cover the pan and sweat gently for about 10 minutes, until the onions are soft and sweet.
3. Add the chicken stock, increase the heat and bring up to a simmer, then add the remaining ingredients and mix everything together well. Remove the pan from the heat and check the seasoning, adjusting if needed.
4. Loosely pack this mixture into a deep lasagne or casserole-style dish and bake in the preheated oven for 25 minutes, until it's a little golden on top.
5. Serve warm, but once cooled it will keep for a few days in a sealed container in the fridge.

DUCK FAT ROAST POTATOES

SERVES 4

1kg floury potatoes (we use Roosters), peeled and cut into even 5cm pieces
a pinch of sea salt
2 teaspoons plain flour
100g duck fat

These sensational roasties have a fan club all their own. Try them and you won't want to have them any other way.

1   Preheat the oven to 180°C. Put a large roasting tray in the oven while it preheats.
2   Put the prepped potatoes in a large saucepan, cover with salted water and bring to a boil. Reduce the heat and simmer, uncovered, for just 2 minutes to blanch.
3   Drain the potatoes in a colander, then put them back in the pan, cover with a lid and shake the pan vigorously to fluff up the outsides. Sprinkle with the flour and shake again for an even coating.
4   Remove the hot roasting tray from the oven and add the duck fat. Pop the tray back in the oven for a few minutes to heat the fat.
5   Use tongs to carefully transfer the potatoes to the hot fat one by one, then turn them over so they are well coated in the fat. Spread them out in a single layer, ensuring they have plenty of room between them for air to circulate.
6   Roast the potatoes in the preheated oven for 40–50 minutes, until crisp and golden, turning each potato at least twice in that time (after 30 minutes when you're taking out the stuffing, then 10 minutes later when you're taking out the Yorkshire puddings.
7   Season generously with salt and serve hot.

VARIATION Replace the duck fat with goose fat for similar results or with 100ml olive oil if you'd prefer to keep it vegetarian, but the oil won't give as crispy a result.

YORKSHIRE PUDDINGS

SERVES 4

2 eggs
90ml milk
110g plain flour
a generous pinch of sea salt
neutral oil

Though not necessarily a classic Irish element in a Sunday roast, a good Yorkshire pudding is a great addition to your plate, especially for mopping up our gravy.

1. Beat the eggs and milk together in a mixing bowl, then transfer to a jug.
2. Sift the flour into the bowl you were just using. Add three-quarters of the liquid mixture to the flour along with a good pinch of salt, stirring to combine – you don't have to whisk it or remove all the lumps, as these will cook out. Stir in the remaining liquid mixture.
3. Transfer to a jug or bowl, cover and leave in the fridge for at least 4 hours or overnight.
4. When you're ready to cook, preheat the oven to 180°C. Heat a deep 4-hole pudding tray (or see the chef's tip) in the oven for at least 10 minutes.
5. Remove the hot tray from the oven and add a good splash of neutral oil in each of the pudding 'cups'. Pour the pudding batter into each cup, filling each one no more than two-thirds full.
6. Return the tray to the preheated oven and bake for 30–35 minutes, until the puddings have puffed up and turned golden brown. Resist opening the door too early while they're cooking to avoid a flat result (check after 25 minutes when you're taking out the stuffing).
7. Serve immediately or allow to cool fully and freeze, then reheat from frozen in a hot oven for 10 minutes.

CHEF'S TIP Ideally, use a deep 4-hole pudding tray to make your Yorkshire puddings. Alternatively, you could use a 12-hole muffin tray and serve a few smaller ones.

CAULIFLOWER CHEESE

SERVES 4, WITH LEFTOVERS

1 large cauliflower, broken into small florets
50g salted butter
4 tablespoons plain flour
500ml cream
100g Cheddar cheese, grated
100g Parmesan cheese, grated
sea salt and ground white pepper
a generous grating of fresh nutmeg or a good pinch of ground nutmeg (about 5g)

This is an old-school family classic elevated with the Parmesan and nutmeg. There will be enough for leftovers too, which is what you want.

1. Preheat the oven to 180°C.
2. Bring a large pot of salted water to a boil. Add the cauliflower florets and blanch for 5 minutes, until just tender. Remove the pan from the heat, strain and set aside to allow the cauliflower to continue cooking in its own heat. (If you'd like to prep this in advance, you can cool the florets quickly by immersing them in cold water and draining well before refrigerating, then just reheat by plunging back into boiling water for 45–60 seconds and straining well before covering in the sauce and baking.)
3. Meanwhile, to make the white sauce, melt the butter in a large heavy-based saucepan over a medium heat. When the butter starts to foam, add the flour, stirring for a minute or two to cook it a little. Whisk in the cream bit by bit, then reduce the heat to low and cook until the sauce has thickened and the flour has cooked out.
4. Remove the pan from the heat and stir in the grated Cheddar and Parmesan. Allow it to melt into the sauce, then season with salt, white pepper and grated nutmeg. (If you want to make this in advance and hold it, be sure to cover the surface directly with cling film to prevent it from forming a skin and keep it somewhere warm.)
5. Transfer the warm cauliflower to a large baking dish, then pour over the warm sauce. Bake in the preheated oven for 30 minutes, until golden and bubbling. Serve hot.

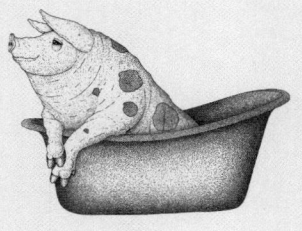

PIES

CHICKEN AND CHORIZO PIE

SERVES 4

1–2 tablespoons neutral oil
1 small white onion, diced
1 leek, white part and a little green only, thinly sliced
2 carrots, diced
2 celery sticks, diced
2 garlic cloves, crushed
1 sprig of fresh thyme
100g fresh chorizo, diced
sea salt and freshly ground black pepper
100ml white wine
20g salted butter
20g plain flour
250–300ml chicken stock (page 199)
300ml cream
300g cooked chicken (see the chef's tip)
zest of 1 lemon
a large handful of fresh parsley leaves, chopped

FOR THE TOPPING:
1–2 rolls of good-quality puff pastry, thawed
1 egg, beaten

TO SERVE:
crisp green salad or steamed green vegetables

This is a great way to use up leftover chicken from your Sunday roast (page 128). A shortcrust or puff pastry lid suits white meat fillings but this could also be topped with a suet pastry (page 201) or a baked potato mash topping (page 203). You can make individual pithivier-style pies (see page 26) or opt for a family-style pie with a choice of toppings.

1. Preheat the oven to 180°C.
2. Heat the oil in a large heavy-based saucepan over a medium-low heat. Add the vegetables, garlic and thyme, cover the pan and sweat for 7–8 minutes, until they begin to soften. Add the chorizo, season with salt and pepper and cook for a further 3–4 minutes, until the chorizo releases some of its oil.
3. Add the white wine and reduce by half. Add the butter and flour and stir to form a light paste. Add 250ml of the chicken stock and reduce by a quarter, then continue to stir as you gradually add the cream.
4. Cook gently for about 10 minutes, until the sauce thickens, stirring occasionally so it doesn't catch. Remove the pan from the heat and allow to cool slightly, then stir in the cooked chicken, lemon zest and parsley.
5. Check the consistency of the sauce, adding the remaining 50ml of stock to loosen if needed.
6. Unroll the puff pastry on a lightly floured surface. Spoon the filling into a pie dish or baking dish, then top with the sheet of pastry, pressing down on the edges to seal before trimming off any excess. Prick the surface several times with a fork. Crimp the edges with the flat tines of the fork or use your thumb or a knife to create scallop shapes. Brush the pastry with the beaten egg.
7. Bake the pie in the preheated oven for 35–40 minutes, until the topping is a rich golden brown and the sides are bubbling. Serve with a crisp green salad or steamed green vegetables on the side.

CHEF'S TIP You'd be surprised how much good chicken meat you can pick off the leftover carcass of a roast. Alternatively, toss three or four chicken breasts or thighs in seasoned flour and bake at 180°C for 30 minutes, then chop or pick the meat and add it to the sauce.

VARIATION If you're using leftover roast chicken, throw a couple of baked potatoes in with your roast to make a baked potato mash topping, which will keep well in the fridge until you want to make this pie midweek. If serving with a potato topping, keep the consistency of the filling quite loose.

DRINK PAIRING With its chilli and ginger heat, our Spicy Lychee cocktail on page 179 makes a good 'like with like' match for the chorizo. – Stephen

BEEF AND GUINNESS PIE

SERVES 8

1kg beef cheek
sea salt and freshly ground black pepper
200g plain flour
1–2 tablespoons neutral oil
500g smoked pork belly, cut into 1cm x 2cm lardons
1 large Spanish onion, chopped
1 leek, sliced
2 large carrots, chopped
1 celery stick, chopped
3–4 large (20g) garlic cloves, chopped
10g fresh thyme, leaves picked
20g tomato purée
500ml red wine
500ml Guinness stout
1 litre beef stock (page 199)
40g blue cheese (we use Cashel Blue)
2 tablespoons Worcestershire sauce

FOR THE PIE TOPPING:
1 batch of suet pastry (page 201)
1 egg, beaten

TO SERVE:
baked potato mash (page 203) and Sunday roast gravy (page 200) or steamed long-stem broccoli

This classic Irish combination of flavours is all about savoury comfort. Source the best local grass-fed beef you can find and look for a nice, rich marbling of fat through the cheek, which is where all that flavour is stored. Pan-roasting the meat is key. Take the time to get a rich sear on the meat and a dark brown coating on the pan, as that's the foundation of all the flavour in your pie.

1. Brine the beef cheek overnight (see page 25).
2. Remove the beef from the brine and pat it dry. Cut into large chunks, season and toss in the flour to coat.
3. Heat the oil in a large heavy-based casserole on a high heat. Working in batches so you don't overcrowd the pot, as you want to sear rather than stew the meat, add the beef and brown it really well, turning to brown each side to a rich, dark colour. Remove from the casserole and set aside.
4. Add the pork belly lardons and cook for a few minutes to render out some of the fat, then add the onion, leek, carrots, celery, garlic and thyme with a little extra oil, if needed. Reduce the heat to medium-high and cook for 5–6 minutes, until golden brown, stirring occasionally to ensure the vegetables don't catch.
5. Add the tomato purée and cook for a further 3 minutes, stirring, then add the wine to deglaze, stirring until the bottom of the pot comes clean. Continue cooking to reduce until the wine has almost completely evaporated. Add the Guinness and reduce by about one-third.
6. Return the meat back to the pot and cover with the beef stock. Bring to a simmer and cook, uncovered, for 2–3 hours over a low heat, until the meat is tender.
7. Remove the meat with a slotted spoon, increase the heat to high and reduce the sauce until it thickens enough to coat the meat. Add the meat back in, stir in the blue cheese and Worcestershire sauce and adjust the seasoning to taste. This pie base can be cooled at this point and refrigerated for up to four days.
8. Preheat the oven to 180°C.
9. Remove the suet pastry from the fridge (and the pie filling too if it was refrigerated ahead of time). Transfer the pie filling to a large pie dish or baking dish.
10. Roll out the pastry on a lightly floured surface to a circle or rectangle that's slightly larger than your chosen dish so that it can be tucked over the edges. Fill the dish with the beef filling, then top with the pastry, pressing in the edges to seal. Prick the surface of the pastry several times with a fork. Crimp the edges of the pastry with the tines of the fork or use your thumb or a knife to create scallop shapes.

11 Brush the pastry generously with the beaten egg. Put the pie dish on a baking tray to catch any drips if the pie filling bubbles up and over a bit. Bake in the preheated oven for 35–40 minutes, until the pastry is a rich golden brown and the sides are bubbling.
12 Serve with mashed potatoes and gravy or steamed long-stem broccoli, depending on your mood.

CHEF'S TIP Melting blue cheese into meaty pies like this adds a layer of savoury umami flavour without giving it a particularly cheesy character.

DRINK PAIRING A pie and a pint? Some days are made for it, and a pint of Guinness (or Guinness 0.0) will hit the spot with this suet pastry pie. – Aoife
For something different, our Château de Cèdre Malbec from Cahors in southern France is layered, textured and delicious. – Denise

SHEPHERD'S PIE

SERVES 6-8

1kg boneless lamb shoulder
sea salt and freshly ground black pepper
2 tablespoons olive oil
500g lamb shoulder mince
2 large onions, diced
4 carrots, diced
2 celery sticks, diced
4 garlic cloves, chopped
4 sprigs of fresh thyme, leaves picked and finely chopped
4 sprigs of fresh rosemary
50g tomato purée
300ml red wine
500ml beef stock (page 199)
2 x 400g tins of good-quality chopped tomatoes
100g red wine jus (page 197; optional)
50ml Worcestershire sauce
50ml Tabasco sauce
juice of 1 lemon
a good pinch of caster sugar
300g frozen peas
100g fresh parsley, leaves picked and chopped

FOR THE TOPPING:
2 egg yolks
750g baked potato mash (page 203)

TO SERVE:
Parmesan cheese, for grating (optional)
brown sauce, shop-bought or homemade (page 194)

This is a hearty and generous-sized pie that's great for a crowd. In a twist on our slow-braised lamb hotpot (see page 86), we use whole chunks of lamb shoulder as well as the usual minced lamb to elevate this luxury shepherd's pie and showcase the quality and flavour of Irish lamb.

1. Cut the lamb shoulder into large chunks, removing any hard fat and sinew. Season with salt and pepper.
2. Heat a large heavy-based casserole over a high heat until it's smoking hot. Add a little olive oil, then add some of the seasoned lamb shoulder chunks. It's important not to overcrowd the pan as you want to sear the meat, not stew it in its own juices, so do this in batches if necessary, adding a little more oil if needed. Make sure to get a good rich colour on all sides of the lamb. Once the chunks are nicely seared, remove and set aside.
3. Now add your lamb mince, season with salt and cook over a high heat, stirring periodically to prevent it catching, until it's dark brown and almost crispy. Remove from the pan and set aside.
4. Reduce the heat to medium-high. Add the onions, carrots, celery, garlic and herbs and cook for 4–5 minutes, until golden. Add the tomato purée and cook out for another 2–3 minutes, then add the wine to deglaze the pan, stirring until the bottom of the pot comes clean, and reduce the wine by half. Add the lamb chunks and mince back in together with the beef stock, chopped tomatoes and red wine jus (if using).
5. Bring to a simmer and cook, uncovered, over a gentle heat for about 4 hours, until very tender, stirring periodically to ensure it doesn't catch. Season with the Worcestershire, Tabasco, lemon juice, sugar and salt and pepper to taste. (You can allow the filling to cool at this stage and refrigerate it for up to three days.)
6. Preheat the oven to 200°C.
7. Stir the frozen peas and fresh parsley through the pie filling, then transfer into a large pie dish or baking dish.
8. Fold the egg yolks through the baked potato mash to help it form a golden crust. Pipe the mash over the pie filling or scoop it over and use a spatula to spread it evenly, then run the tines of a fork along the mash to help it crisp up.
9. Put the pie dish on a baking tray to catch any drips if the filling bubbles up and over a bit. Bake in the preheated oven for 35–40 minutes, until golden on top and bubbling up at the sides.
10. Grate over some fresh Parmesan cheese (if using) and serve with brown sauce on the side.

VARIATION Swap out the lamb shoulder called for here with 800g of cooked, slow-braised lamb shoulder (page 86). Cook the mince for 2 hours, then add the braised shoulder.

DRINK PAIRING Cabernet-led Bordeaux is a classic pairing for roast lamb but it would also work brilliantly with this luxurious spin on a shepherd's pie. Treat yourself with a Saint-Estèphe from Château Phélan Ségur. – Denise

FISH PIE

SERVES 4-6

20 cooked mussels, meat picked (or see step 3 if using uncooked)
a generous splash of white wine
sea salt and freshly ground black pepper
1 monkfish tail, cut into thumb-sized chunks (about 25g each)
200g salmon, cut into thumb-sized chunks (about 25g each)
100g smoked haddock, cut into thumb-sized chunks (about 25g each)
10 fresh Atlantic prawns, peeled and cut into thirds
50g frozen peas
5 spring onions, thinly sliced
a handful of fresh chives, chopped

FOR THE WHITE SAUCE:

700ml milk
1 bay leaf
75g salted butter
55g plain flour
2 tablespoons lemon juice
200g onion, finely chopped
100ml white wine
100ml double cream
50g Gruyère cheese, grated
50g Parmesan cheese, grated

FOR THE PARSLEY CRUMB TOPPING:

50g panko breadcrumbs
50g Gruyère cheese, grated
50g Parmesan cheese, grated
a handful of chopped fresh parsley
1 garlic clove, finely chopped
2 teaspoons lemon zest
1 tablespoon olive oil

You can change up the fish that you use in this pie but the important thing is to have lots of contrasts of colour, texture, shape and flavour and not to overpower with any one fish.

1. Preheat the oven to 180°C.
2. Cook the potatoes as per the recipe for baked potato mash on page 203.
3. If you're using fresh uncooked mussels, prep them as per the pil pil recipe on page 114. Heat a large heavy-based saucepan over a high heat until it's smoking hot. Add the mussels and a generous splash of wine, cover and cook for 3-4 minutes, until all the mussels open (discard any that remain closed). Allow to cool, pick the meat and refrigerate until ready to use.
4. To make the white sauce, put the milk and bay leaf in a medium-sized saucepan and bring to a boil, then immediately remove the pan from the heat.
5. In a separate large saucepan, melt 45g butter over a low heat. When the butter starts to foam, add the flour and cook for 5 minutes, stirring continuously. Gradually pour in the hot milk, stirring constantly. Reduce the heat to low, add the lemon juice, season with salt and pepper to taste and simmer for 8 minutes.
6. Meanwhile, melt the remaining 30g butter in a separate frying pan over a low heat. When the butter starts to foam, add the onion, cover the pan and sweat for 5 minutes, until softened and translucent. Add the wine, bring back to a simmer and continue to cook until the liquid has reduced by two-thirds, then add the cream.
7. Remove the bay leaf from the milk sauce, then stir in the onion mixture and the grated cheeses. Set aside. (You can make this an hour or two in advance but cover the surface directly with cling film to prevent a skin from forming and hold it in a warm place.)
8. To make the topping, combine the breadcrumbs, cheeses, parsley, garlic and zest in a large mixing bowl, drizzle in the olive oil and season well. Set aside. (If making this in advance, hold the oil until ready to use.)
9. To season the monkfish and salmon (but not the smoked haddock, which is already salted), either brine it for 15 minutes (see page 25) or cover it lightly with fine sea salt, sit it on large plate for 30 minutes to firm up a little and pat it dry before using.
10. Once the potatoes are baked, mash them as per the instructions on page 203, season generously with salt, white pepper and the nutmeg, cover and set aside somewhere warm.
11. In a large mixing bowl, combine the seasoned fish with the smoked haddock, cooked mussels and prawns. Stir in the white sauce along with the peas, spring onions and chives and season well. Transfer to a large pie dish or baking dish.

FOR THE TOPPING:
500g baked potato mash (page 203)
sea salt and ground white pepper
¼ teaspoon ground nutmeg
2 egg yolks

TO SERVE:
Guinness brown bread (page 64; optional)

12 At the last minute, fold the egg yolks through the mash topping to help it form a lovely golden crust. Pipe the mash over the pie filling or scoop it over and use a spatula to spread it evenly, then run the tines of a fork along the mash topping to help it crisp up. Top with the parsley crumb.
13 Put the pie dish on a baking tray to catch any drips if the filling bubbles up and over a bit. Bake in the preheated oven for 35–40 minutes, until the mash turns golden around the sides and the sauce is bubbling up at the sides.
14 Serve on its own or with Guinness brown bread on the side.

DRINK PAIRING Hope Beer's Underdog Pilsner is a clean, crisp lager made with German lager yeast, with Hallertauer Mittelfrüh and Saaz hops bringing a refreshing bitterness to balance the subtle malt sweetness. – Stephen

DESSERTS

WHITE CHOCOLATE AND RASPBERRY CRÈME BRÛLÉE

SERVES 6–8

550ml cream
100g good-quality white chocolate, broken into pieces
1 vanilla pod, split in half lengthways and seeds scraped out, or 1 teaspoon vanilla extract
6 egg yolks
2 tablespoons caster sugar, plus extra for the topping
1 punnet of fresh raspberries
tiny fresh mint sprigs, to serve

This is a perfect summer dessert, full of flavour but light enough that it doesn't feel too heavy at the end of a three-course meal. You can keep it easy and serve this without the brûlée topping, but if you have a kitchen blowtorch at home, this is a fun way to finish the dish.

1. Preheat the oven to 160°C.
2. Gently heat the cream in a small saucepan over a medium-low heat, then add the white chocolate. Add the vanilla seeds and the scraped-out pod (if using) to infuse or add the vanilla extract. Stir until the chocolate is melted and remove from the heat.
3. In a large mixing bowl, whisk the egg yolks and sugar together until slightly fluffy. Remove the vanilla pod (if using) from the cream, then gradually pour in the hot cream, stirring to incorporate.
4. Divide the mixture among six to eight ramekins, depending on their size and how many you want to serve. Pop a few raspberries in each one.
5. Put the ramekins in a deep roasting tray and pour in enough warm water to reach halfway up the sides of the ramekins. Transfer to the preheated oven and cook for about 20 minutes, until set with just the slightest wobble in the centre.
6. Remove from the oven and allow to cool before refrigerating until ready to serve. These will keep for up to four days in the fridge.
7. Remove the ramekins from the fridge 20 minutes before serving to return to room temperature.
8. Dab away any moisture from the surface with some kitchen paper, then sprinkle evenly with caster sugar (about 1½ teaspoons per ramekin), using the back of the spoon to spread it evenly.
9. Using a kitchen blowtorch, carefully caramelise all the sugar, keeping the flame moving so that you don't burn the sugar in any one area. The sugar will cook into a caramel-coloured glaze that will harden into a crispy caramel lid. (Alternatively, see the chef's tip if you don't have a kitchen blowtorch.) Return to the fridge for 10 minutes to chill before serving.
10. Serve with a few fresh raspberries and a tiny sprig of mint on top.

CHEF'S TIP If you don't have a blowtorch, don't be tempted to try this under the grill as you won't get crispy enough results. Instead, serve it slightly chilled with a shortbread biscuit on the side to add the texture contrast.

DRINK PAIRING If you're unconvinced that dessert wine can be a perfect end to a rich meal, try the Mount Horrocks 'Cordon Cut' Riesling from Australia's Clare Valley, with its tightrope balance of luscious ripe fruit and acidity. – Aoife

CHOCOLATE AND PISTACHIO TART

SERVES 8

50g high-quality dark chocolate (70% cocoa solids)
50g salted butter, plus extra for greasing
1 egg, beaten
55g caster sugar
45g plain flour
1 teaspoon (5g) cocoa powder

FOR THE PISTACHIO PASTE:
35g caster sugar
35g boiling water
100g shelled pistachios

FOR THE GANACHE:
300g high-quality dark chocolate (70% cocoa solids), roughly chopped
500ml cream

TO SERVE:
good-quality ice cream of choice
honeycomb crumb (page 213 or you could cheat with a roughly chopped Crunchie bar)

We serve this tart with roast banana ice cream from Scúp Gelato in Wexford, who won a coveted Golden Fork at the Great Taste Awards in 2022. It's a great contrast for the rich tart.

1. Preheat the oven to 200°C.
2. Set a heatproof bowl over a pot of simmering water (a bain-marie; see page 24), making sure the water doesn't touch the bottom of the bowl. Add the chocolate and allow it to melt gently, then add the butter and stir until that has melted too.
3. In another large bowl, whisk together the egg and sugar to make a fluffy cream. Add the melted chocolate and butter little by little, stirring to incorporate evenly. Sieve in the flour and cocoa powder and mix until it comes together into a rough ball.
4. Grease a 23cm loose-bottomed tart tin and lightly flour a clean surface and rolling pin.
5. Working from the inside out, roll the dough into a circle big enough to cover the tin with a little extra at the sides. Put the dough in the tin, pushing it into the corners and leaving a little overhang. Line the tart base with a piece of non-stick baking paper, fill with baking beans and transfer to the preheated oven to blind bake for 4–5 minutes, until it starts to firm up and develop a bit of a crust. Remove from the oven and allow the beans to cool a little before removing.
6. Meanwhile, to make the pistachio paste, dissolve the sugar in the boiling water to make a syrup. Combine with the pistachios and blitz in a high-speed blender to form a paste. If it's too dry you can add a splash of cream, but not too much, just enough to make a paste.
7. Once the tart base is cool to touch, spread the paste evenly over it. (If the base is too hot, the paste won't spread easily).
8. To make the ganache, melt the chocolate in a clean heatproof bowl set over a pan of simmering water, as before, again making sure the water doesn't touch the bottom of the bowl. Pour in the cream and stir until smooth. Pour the ganache over the pistachio paste and refrigerate for at least 1 hour to set before serving. This will keep well in the fridge for up to five days.
9. Serve at room temperature with your ice cream of choice and some honeycomb crumb scattered over.

DRINK PAIRING For dark chocolate, a red dessert wine is a classic go-to. Try the sweet Château de Cèdre Malbec to see for yourself. – Izzy

A well-made port would be a treat with this chocolate tart, whether a young, fresh and fruit-forward ruby port (try Niepoort's) or an aged LBV like the Quinta do Noval LBV Port 2013 on The Old Spot list. – Aoife

STICKY TOFFEE PUDDING

SERVES 6

240g whole pitted dates (the best quality you can find), roughly chopped
250ml water
1 tea bag of black tea
35g bread soda
140g salted butter, softened, plus extra for greasing
140g muscovado sugar
3 eggs
150g plain flour

FOR THE TOFFEE SAUCE:
175g muscovado sugar
60g salted butter
240g double cream
40g treacle

TO SERVE:
fresh or whipped cream or good-quality vanilla ice cream

This is a favourite of Alisa Pop, our reservations manager. It's a true comfort classic of a dessert, just the thing to enjoy in our cosy gastropub or to bring that cosiness into your own home.

1. Preheat the oven to 160°C. Grease a 23cm square baking dish.
2. Combine the dates and water in a saucepan with the tea bag and 20g of the bread soda. Bring to a boil, then reduce the heat and simmer for 15 minutes. Once the dates are soft, remove the tea bag and discard, then blend the mixture into a paste and scrape out into a large bowl. Set aside.
3. In a large mixing bowl, beat the butter and sugar together to make a creamy paste. Add the eggs and beat again until blended.
4. Fold this egg mixture into the date mixture, then sieve in the flour and the remaining 15g bread soda and fold it in to form a smooth batter.
5. Transfer to the greased baking dish and smooth the top. Bake in the preheated oven for 45 minutes, until a skewer inserted in the centre comes out clean.
6. Meanwhile, to make the toffee sauce, melt the sugar in a pan over a low heat, watching carefully so it doesn't burn. When a golden syrup has formed, add the butter and allow it to gently foam and bubble, without stirring, until combined. Slowly add the cream, stirring to incorporate, and reduce until a caramel consistency has formed. Add the treacle and cook for another minute, stirring. Remove from the heat and set aside or refrigerate until ready to use. This will last for at least a week in the fridge.
7. Remove the cooked pudding from the oven and prick all over with a skewer, then pour over one-third of the sauce. Cover the remaining sauce with a lid or cartouche (see page 25) and set them both aside somewhere warm for 15 minutes before spooning out servings family style, with the extra sauce poured over and fresh or whipped cream or good-quality vanilla ice cream on top or on the side.

VARIATION For individual servings, remove the cooked pudding from the oven and allow to cool before turning it out onto a board and cutting into neat portion-sized squares. Refrigerate for up to four days. Reheat on a baking tray with the sauce poured over in a preheated oven at 140°C for 9 minutes.

DRINK PAIRING Our Banana Mai Tai on page 188 has lots of complementary flavours but also the acidity to cut the richness of the pudding. – Izzy

A chilled 10-year-old tawny port will offer caramel, honey and toffee notes to complement the sauce in this classic pudding. We love Niepoort's complex version. – Stephen

BREAD AND BUTTER PUDDING

SERVES 4–6

30g salted butter
250ml milk
250ml cream
50g white chocolate, roughly broken or chopped
1 vanilla pod, halved lengthways
zest of 1 orange
2 eggs
50g caster sugar
1 x 400g brioche loaf, sliced

TO SERVE:
good-quality vanilla ice cream

Who doesn't love a bread and butter pudding – especially when it's made extra-luxurious with brioche, white chocolate and the brightness of orange zest?

1. Preheat the oven to 180°C. Grease a large baking tray, dish or standard 900g (2lb) loaf tin with the butter.
2. Combine the milk and cream in a saucepan and heat gently, then add the white chocolate and stir to melt. Remove the pan from the heat, scrape in the seeds from the vanilla pod and add the orange zest.
3. Whisk the eggs and sugar together in a large heatproof mixing bowl. Place this over a pan of gently simmering water, making sure the water doesn't touch the bottom of the bowl, to create a bain-marie (see page 24). Gradually add the hot milk and cream, stirring over this gentle heat until you reach a custard consistency.
4. Layer up the sliced brioche in the greased baking dish and pour over the custard. Allow to soak for 15 minutes, then bake in the preheated oven for 40 minutes.
5. Remove from the oven and serve hot with vanilla ice cream.

VARIATION You could leave out the melted white chocolate and add chocolate buttons when layering up the brioche or swap out the brioche for panettone with chocolate chips or dried fruit.

DRINK PAIRING Frangelico hazelnut liqueur simply poured over plenty of well-made ice (see page 171) is an elegant, old-school match for these vanilla, orange and white chocolate flavours. – Aoife

YOGURT PANNA COTTA WITH BLOOD ORANGE JELLY AND GINGER CRUMB

SERVES 4

500ml cream
1 vanilla pod, halved lengthways
100g caster sugar
3½ gelatine leaves
300g Greek-style yogurt

FOR THE BLOOD ORANGE JELLY:

2½ gelatine leaves
50g caster sugar
50ml hot water
150ml freshly squeezed blood orange juice (2–3 blood oranges)

FOR THE MASCARPONE CREAM:

90g mascarpone cheese
90ml cream
2 teaspoons icing sugar
1 vanilla pod, halved lengthways and seeds scraped out

FOR THE GINGER CRUMB:

2 tablespoons ginger syrup, shop-bought or homemade (page 211)
50g salted butter
80g caster sugar
40g plain flour
1 teaspoon ground ginger
1 teaspoon bread soda
a pinch of sea salt
1 egg, beaten
zest of 1 orange

This dessert is as pretty as it is delicious. The combination of warming ginger and bittersweet blood oranges is welcome in the late winter and early spring months, when blood oranges are in season.

1. Pour the cream into a saucepan set over a medium heat. Scrape the vanilla seeds into the cream, then add the scraped-out pod too. Add the sugar and stir to dissolve fully, then remove the pan from the heat.
2. Meanwhile, soak the gelatine leaves in a little cold water for 5 minutes. Once softened, lift them out of the water and add them to the warm cream. Whisk to dissolve fully, then set aside and allow to cool completely.
3. Combine the infused cream with the yogurt and mix well to fully incorporate, then pour this mixture into four containers of choice. You can set and serve the panna cotta in ramekins or use four individual glass bowls or tumblers so that you can see the layers for presentation. Refrigerate for at least 4 hours to set. This will keep well in the fridge for up to four days.
4. To make the jelly, soak the gelatine in a little cold water for 5 minutes. Dissolve the sugar in the hot water in a medium-sized bowl, then add the softened gelatine and whisk to dissolve fully. Add the orange juice, then pour into a large tray and allow to cool at room temperature for 45–60 minutes. It needs to cool to room temperature but remain at a pouring consistency, so don't leave it for more than an hour or it will be too firm.
5. Pour a layer of jelly over the fully set panna cotta. Return to the fridge for at least 2 hours to set the jelly.
6. Meanwhile, combine the mascarpone and cream, then add the icing sugar and scrape in the vanilla seeds. Mix well and refrigerate until ready to use.
7. To make the ginger crumb, preheat the oven to 180°C. Grease or line a baking tray with non-stick baking paper.
8. In a small saucepan, combine the ginger syrup and butter over a gentle heat, stirring until they are melted together.
9. In a large mixing bowl, combine the sugar, flour, ground ginger, bread soda and a pinch of salt. Drizzle in the butter-syrup mixture, then add the egg and orange zest and beat to incorporate.
10. Pour this mixture into the prepared tray, then bake in the preheated oven for 20 minutes, until golden brown and biscuit-textured. Remove from the oven and allow to cool before breaking up into a loose, rough crumb. This will keep well in a sealed container for a week or two and can be used to garnish anything from poached fruit with ice cream to cheesecake or even granola.
11. To serve, top each panna cotta with a quenelle (see page 26) of mascarpone cream and scatter over some ginger crumb.

DRINK PAIRING Pick up on the blood orange flavours with the citrussy Amaretto Sour on page 188. – Aoife

JAFFA CAKE

SERVES 8

40g high-quality dark chocolate (70% cocoa solids), roughly chopped or buttons
40g unsalted butter
15g caster sugar
1 egg
1 egg yolk
45g plain flour
1 teaspoon (5g) cocoa powder

FOR THE CHOCOLATE CUSTARD:

270g high-quality chocolate caramel buttons (available online; we use Callebaut)
230g high-quality dark chocolate (70% cocoa solids), roughly chopped or buttons
300ml cream
200ml milk
a pinch of salt
3 medium eggs, beaten

FOR THE CHOCOLATE MOUSSE:

120g caster sugar
35ml cold water
150g high-quality dark chocolate (64% cocoa solids), roughly chopped or buttons
3 egg yolks
2 teaspoons (10g) caster sugar
90ml cream

Jaffa Cake biscuits were as much a part of growing up in Ireland as Quality Street sweets and red lemonade. This dessert captures those orange and chocolate flavours and spongy textures in a grown-up, crowd-pleasing tart.

1. Preheat the oven to 180°C. Lightly grease a loose-bottomed tart tin (23cm wide x 5cm high) and lightly flour a clean surface and rolling pin.
2. Set a heatproof bowl over a pot of simmering water (a bain-marie – see page 24), making sure the water doesn't touch the bottom of the bowl. Add the chocolate and allow it to melt gently, then add the butter and stir until that has melted and is well combined.
3. Meanwhile, in another bowl or stand mixer, whisk together the sugar, egg and yolk to make a fluffy cream with a soft peak consistency. Add the melted chocolate and butter little by little, stirring to incorporate evenly. Mix for another minute or two to bring everything together. Sieve in the flour and cocoa powder and mix until it comes together into a rough ball.
4. Working from the inside out, roll the dough into a circle big enough to cover the tin with a little extra at the sides. Put the dough in the tin, pushing it into the corners and leaving a little overhang. Line the tart base with a piece of non-stick baking paper, fill with baking beans and transfer to the preheated oven to blind bake for 4–5 minutes, until it starts to firm up and develop a bit of a crust. Remove from the oven and allow the beans to cool a little before removing. Allow the base to cool fully.
5. Meanwhile, to make the custard, break the chocolate caramel buttons and dark chocolate into a large heatproof bowl. Combine the cream, milk and salt in a saucepan and bring to a simmer, then pour this hot liquid over the chocolate and stir until melted. Add the beaten eggs and stir until smooth and fully incorporated.
6. Pour the custard into the tart tin over the cooled base, then return it to the oven to cook for 45 minutes, until set with just a slight wobble. Remove from the oven and allow to cool.
7. To make the chocolate mousse, start by making a light caramel. Combine the sugar and water in a heavy-based saucepan and stir with a wooden spoon over a gentle heat until dissolved. Increase the heat to medium and bring it to a gentle boil, without stirring, until it turns a light golden colour. Keep a close eye on it to catch it before it cooks any further.
8. Meanwhile, set up another bain-marie as above and melt the chocolate. Once the caramel is ready, add it to the melted chocolate and stir to combine well. Remove the bowl from the pan and set aside to cool fully.

FOR THE ORANGE JELLY:
5 gelatine leaves
1.5 litres orange juice
50g caster sugar
½ teaspoon orange oil (available in gourmet stores or online)

FOR THE CHOCOLATE GLAZE:
7 gelatine leaves
300g caster sugar
100g cocoa powder
400ml cream
50ml milk
100g high-quality dark chocolate (70% cocoa solids), roughly chopped or buttons

9. Put a second bowl over the pan as another bain-marie. Add the egg yolks and sugar and whisk for about 3 minutes, until it forms a sabayon (a light, frothy, creamy consistency). Fold the sabayon into the cooled chocolate mixture.
10. Whip the cream to a soft peak consistency, then fold this into the mixture to create the chocolate mousse.
11. To construct the dessert, add a layer of chocolate mousse on top of the cooled, cooked custard. Put in the fridge for 30 minutes to set.
12. Meanwhile, to make the orange jelly, soak the gelatine in a small bowl with a little cold water for about 10 minutes.
13. In a medium-sized saucepan, heat the orange juice to a rolling simmer to reduce by half. Add the sugar, and orange oil, stirring to dissolve the sugar. Pour the cold water off the gelatine, add a little of the hot orange liquid and stir to melt the gelatine. Add this to the orange liquid and allow to cool completely.
14. Once cool, pour a thin layer of jelly over the mousse and return to the fridge for another 30 minutes to finish setting.
15. To make the chocolate glaze, soak the gelatine in a small bowl with a little cold water for 10 minutes.
16. Meanwhile, combine the sugar, cocoa powder, cream and milk in a saucepan and bring to a simmer. Add the chocolate and stir to melt. Pour the cold water off the gelatine, add a little of the hot chocolate and stir to melt the gelatine. Add this to the hot chocolate, mix together and allow to cool completely.
17. To finish constructing the dessert, top it off with the chocolate glaze and put in the fridge for at least an hour before serving. This will keep well in the fridge for at least a day or two.

DRINK PAIRING Stay classic with a nice cup of tea or indulge in an aged Irish whiskey like the under-appreciated Yellow Spot, a 12-year-old single pot still with Malaga and sherry cask flavours. – Aoife

CHEESE, CRACKERS, CHUTNEY

We change up our cheese fairly regularly at The Old Spot but usually serve a mix of Irish and French farmhouse cheese. A good cheeseboard will offer a contrast of flavours and textures, so you can play around with whatever is available. Consider using at least one hard cheese, one soft or semi-soft cheese and one blue cheese. Different milk flavours can offer a welcome contrast too, such as including a goat or sheep milk cheese in your selection. Our latest favourites are:

- **HARD:** 18-month aged Comté, a French Alpine cow's milk cheese aged for 18 months to intensify the nutty, savoury notes that layer over its sweet, fruity flavours.
- **SOFT:** Killeen Goat, a fresh and clean-tasting Gouda-style semi-soft cheese made near Portumna, Co. Galway by Dutch-born cheesemaker Marion Roeleveld.
- **BLUE:** Wicklow Blue, a mild, creamy blue cheese made from cow's milk in a Brie style with a bloomy rind.

We serve our cheese with fresh grapes, chutney and sometimes quince jelly (membrillo). We like to switch up the chutneys, with favourites including burnt orange; apricot; pear and apple; and plum chutney (page 210). Our apricot purée (page 209) would also make for a nice, sweet contrast, especially with the creamy Wicklow Blue.

We like to serve a variety of artisan rye and wholemeal crackers, but thinly sliced sourdough, either fresh or toasted, works well too.

CHEF'S TIP When storing your cheese in the fridge, be sure to keep each cheese individually wrapped in greaseproof paper in a well-sealed container. Always take the cheese out of the fridge at least 2–3 hours before serving to bring it to room temperature.

VARIATION Instead of serving a cheeseboard with a selection of different cheeses, it can be nice to choose a single seasonal treat, like a whole baked Mont d'Or in winter. Just pierce a hole in the top, pour in a small splash of white wine and push in a sprig of rosemary or thyme, then bake in the oven for 20 minutes at 180°C before serving with a warm baguette or crusty bread. This works equally well with a Camembert or Irish Cavanbert from Silke Cropp in Co. Cavan.

DRINK PAIRING A white Burgundy from Irish winemaker Róisín Curley would make a classy pairing for Irish farmhouse cheese. Her floral Bourgogne Aligoté shows what Burgundy's other white grape can do in the right hands. – Denise

An apple brandy would make a lovely match for the creamy blue cheese in particular. Our Château du Breuil Calvados from Pays d'Auge is a fine 12-year-old example. – Stephen

COCKTAILS

WE LOVE COCKTAILS at The Old Spot: creating them, making them, serving them, drinking them. We like to play around with new twists on old classics in our regularly changing cocktail list and on our Cocktail of the Week blackboard and were proud to be shortlisted for the Best Cocktail Experience at the Irish Restaurant Awards 2022.

We make lots of our own fruit purées and infusions – of sugar syrups, spirits and even non-alcoholic spirits. There are good-quality brands of purées and flavoured syrups or spirits available to buy, but making your own allows you to get creative. From a home bar perspective, it also keeps costs down.

Mix up a blueberry syrup and our Blue Blood Bramble (with Gordon's Mediterranean Orange Gin, crème de mûre, blueberry syrup and lemon juice) becomes a breeze. Batch up a chilli-infused tequila and you have the basis for our Spicy Lychee, sweetened with hibiscus, ginger and lychee, then sharpened with lime juice and cranberry juice.

We've shared some of our favourite infusions, syrups, garnishes and cocktail recipes but feel free to play around with your own combinations. There are no hard and fast rules in terms of ratios of flavours, so trust your palate and taste as you go (with the exception of hot syrups – safety first, folks! – so be sure the liquid you're tasting is cool).

Remember, too, that there are usually a few different ways of achieving similar results. For example, in a professional bar, batching a blood orange gin is more efficient than keeping blood oranges in fresh supply and muddling every time, but if you have them fresh at home, then muddling might be the quickest, easiest approach for you. Likewise, we make a cucumber syrup and ginger syrup for our Old Spot signature cocktail, but in the recipe on page 177 we've suggested that you muddle the fresh ingredients instead.

Experiment, taste as you go (use a straw) and pay attention to the results so you can tweak it next time, just as you would when cooking food, only arguably more fun!

INFUSIONS

We like to infuse neutral spirits to make our own citrus-flavoured gins and vodkas, like a blood orange gin for The Old Spot cocktail on page 177 or a grapefruit-infused Istil 38 vodka for It's Sunny Somewhere on page 182. Tequila is excellent infused with chilli peppers: simply slice five or six fresh red chillies lengthways and add to 700ml tequila, seeds and all. For banana-infused rum, slice a bunch of very ripe, brown bananas and infuse in 700ml rum in a sterilised Kilner jar (see page 26) for up to six weeks.

For infusing 0.0% spirits, we slice the citrus thinly, dehydrate the slices at 60°C for 18 hours (see the next page) and infuse them in the spirit for at least 24 hours or up to a week. A handful of dehydrated slices should be enough for a 700ml bottle. We also infuse Gordons 0.0 with fresh vanilla pods (2–3 per 700ml), sliced lengthways down the centre and popped into the bottle for at least a day to infuse.

We recommend leaving all infusions for at least 24 hours before using but ideally about a week. The longer you leave it, the stronger the results, so taste it as you go.

Infused spirits and syrups can be stored at room temperature, as both alcohol and sugar will preserve the added ingredients, though a cool, dark space is best for keeping the flavours fresh. Infused alcoholic-free liquids like Gordon's 0.0 are best stored in the fridge.

If storing herb infusions for any longer than a week, it's best to strain the liquid through a fine mesh sieve and discard the leaves before they start to blacken.

SYRUPS

Most cocktail recipes require a sugar syrup of some sort. These are usually made with a ratio of 1:1 sugar to hot water, as per the recipes on page 172, or 2:1 for a thicker, more concentrated syrup.

DEHYDRATED FRUIT

We get great use out of our dehydrator and regularly dehydrate slices of lime, grapefruit or blood oranges to use as a garnish or for infusing our 0.0% spirits.

You can pick up a dehydrator at affordable prices, then dehydrate at 60°C for 18 hours for citrus fruit, 12 hours for sliced chilli peppers or 6–8 hours for sliced banana (great for garnishes). These will keep well in an airtight container for at least a month.

Alternatively, you could experiment at home with an air fryer or by dehydrating fruit slices in an oven at 120°C for 1 hour.

A WORD ON ICE

Not all ice is made equally, so it's a good idea to consider what you want your ice to do.

Crushed ice makes a cocktail extra refreshing, adding a slushy texture and diluting it a little to soften the spirits. Simply put some ice in the centre of a clean tea towel, wrap it up and use a hammer or mallet to crush it. Alternatively, put the ice in a ziplock bag and bash it with a rolling pin or briefly blitz some ice cubes in a blender and strain well before using, as the heat of the motor might melt some of the ice.

Sometimes dilution is not desired, however, as in booze-forward cocktails, where a large ice ball or cube will melt slower and keep your drink cool for longer. You can buy moulds for these in good kitchen shops or online.

Sometimes you do want dilution, if not too much. Use standard ice cubes for cocktails that require stirring, allowing a little dilution to loosen and release the flavours and aromas in the spirits. Shaking over ice will dilute the drink more due to the friction while also aerating it and adding some texture.

Finally, when cooling bottles of wine or bubbles in an ice bucket, don't forget to add some water to the bucket to help conduct those cold temperatures fast. And remember that adding salt to the iced water will help cool it down even faster.

SUGAR SYRUP

MAKES ABOUT 250ML

200g granulated or caster sugar
200ml hot water

1. Dissolve the sugar in the hot water. If using as is, allow to cool before adding to a cocktail or store somewhere cool and dry.

VARIATION You can infuse the syrup by adding your choice of the following to 250ml of hot syrup and allowing to cool, then cover and refrigerate for 24 hours to infuse. If not using within a week, strain into a sterilised bottle (see page 26).

- **HERBS:** A few large sprigs of fresh rosemary, thyme, mint, basil or whatever you fancy.
- **SPICES:** Sweet spices like one fresh vanilla pod, split open; or hot spices like two chilli peppers, halved lengthways; a thumb-sized piece of ginger, sliced; or 1 teaspoon of black or pink peppercorns.
- **FRUIT:** A small handful of dehydrated citrus slices like orange, lemon, lime or grapefruit; fresh berries like strawberries, raspberries or blueberries (a generous handful, roughly chopped, and strained after 24 hours); or other soft fruits like watermelon (a generous slice, roughly chopped, and strained after 24 hours).

Alternatively, you can flavour your simple syrup with a fruit tea such as hibiscus (as we do for our Spicy Lychee), raspberry, apple and cinnamon, lemon, etc. Make the tea good and strong by infusing the tea bag in about 100ml of boiling water. Add an extra 100g sugar to the basic syrup to keep the ratio of liquid to sugar correct.

SALTED CARAMEL SYRUP

200g granulated sugar
3 pinches of sea salt
a splash of water

1. Combine the sugar, salt and a small splash of water in a saucepan over a low heat. Stir to combine, then leave it to bubble away very gently for 5–10 minutes, keeping a close eye on it to make sure it doesn't burn. Allow to cool fully before tasting as hot sugar can burn badly.

PASSIONFRUIT PURÉE

15 passionfruit
150ml hot sugar syrup (page 172)
150ml honey

1   Halve the passionfruit and scrape the seeds into a blender. Add the hot sugar syrup and honey, blend and pass through a fine mesh sieve. Keep in the fridge for up to two weeks.

VARIATION Use the same method above to experiment with all sorts of fruit, from kiwis and berries to stone fruit like fresh peaches and apricots.

ULTIMATE G&T

All gin lovers have their own personal preference when it comes to the best gin and tonic, which is why we pride ourselves on offering the ultimate G&T selection, with over a dozen serves to choose from. We pour 50ml measures of gin, topped with a paired choice from the London Essence Company range of tonic waters and soda, and finished with a carefully paired garnish over plenty of ice in a stemmed balloon glass to amplify all the aromatics.

Blackwater Strawberry Gin with London Essence Pomelo & Pink Pepper Tonic Water garnished with a slice of lime and a fresh strawberry

Bombay Sapphire East Gin with London Essence Original Indian Tonic Water garnished with a slice of lime, a twist of lemon peel and a pinch of freshly ground black pepper

Bombay Sapphire Gin with London Essence Original Indian Tonic Water garnished with a slice of lime

Bonac 24 Gin with London Essence Grapefruit & Rosemary Tonic Water garnished with fresh raspberries and a sprig of fresh mint

Brockmans Intensely Smooth Gin with London Essence Ginger Ale garnished with a slice of lemon, fresh blackberries and raspberries

Citadelle Gin de France with London Essence Original Indian Tonic Water garnished with a slice of lime and edible flowers

Dingle Original Gin with London Essence Blood Orange & Elderflower Tonic Water garnished with a slice of orange and a sprig of fresh rosemary

Drumshanbo Gunpowder Irish Gin with London Essence Grapefruit & Rosemary Tonic Water garnished with a slice of grapefruit and a sprig of fresh rosemary

Ha'penny Dublin Dry Gin with London Essence Original Indian Tonic Water garnished with a slice of lemon, fresh blackberries and a twist of lemon peel

Ha'penny Dublin Dry Gin with London Essence White Peach & Jasmine Soda garnished with a slice of orange, fresh blackberries and a twist of orange peel

Hendrick's Gin with London Essence Pomelo & Pink Pepper Tonic Water garnished with a slice of cucumber and a pinch of freshly ground black pepper

Monkey 47 Gin with London Essence Blood Orange & Elderflower Tonic Water garnished with a grating of orange zest and a sprig of fresh rosemary

Plymouth Sloe Gin with London Essence Delicate Ginger Ale garnished with fresh raspberries and strawberries and a slice of lemon

Siegfried Rheinland Dry Gin with London Essence Pomelo & Pink Pepper Tonic Water garnished with a cinnamon stick and slices of orange and grapefruit

Tanqueray London Dry Gin with London Essence Grapefruit & Rosemary Tonic Water garnished with a slice of grapefruit and a sprig of fresh rosemary

Tanqueray No. Ten Gin with London Essence Original Indian Tonic Water garnished with slices of grapefruit and lime

THE OLD SPOT

MAKES 1

2 slices of blood orange
25ml gin
25ml lychee liqueur
40ml apple juice
25ml lime juice
15ml rosemary sugar syrup (page 172)
ice cubes, for shaking and serving

TO GARNISH:
crushed ice (page 171)
1 sprig of fresh rosemary
1 fresh or dehydrated lime wheel
a small straw

If you'd like to make our signature cocktail at home, simply muddle some fresh blood orange into your gin of choice. If you love it (you will) and would like to make lots more of these (we do), then you could infuse your own blood orange gin (see page 170) or pick up one of the many brands that sell it. The apple and rosemary notes make this a great match with our Andarl Farm free-range pork chops with cider jus on page 106.

1. In the base of a cocktail shaker, muddle the slices of blood orange with the gin. (If you're using a blood orange-infused gin, then skip the muddling step and simply add the flavoured gin in the next step.)
2. Add the lychee liqueur, apple and lime juice and sugar syrup to the shaker, shake well over ice and strain into a tumbler over ice, then top up with crushed ice.
3. Garnish with fresh rosemary, a wheel of lime and a small straw.

THE GREEN DOOR

MAKES 1

2 slices of cucumber
½ thumb-sized piece of fresh ginger, sliced
25ml sugar syrup (page 172)
40ml Method & Madness gin
25ml lemon juice
20ml Martini dry vermouth
ice cubes, for shaking

TO GARNISH:
1 strip of fresh cucumber
freshly ground black pepper

This is the cocktail that got us shortlisted for the Best Cocktail Experience at the Irish Restaurant Awards 2022. It makes a gorgeous pairing with our bluefin tuna starter on page 36.

1. For the fresh cucumber strip, peel a full length of cucumber all the way down, roll it into a spiral and spear with a cocktail stick to keep it in place.
2. Grind some black pepper onto a saucer and dip the rim or side of a chilled coupe glass into the pepper to garnish (or you can simply sprinkle the finished cocktail with black pepper before serving).
3. In the base of a cocktail shaker, muddle the slices of cucumber and ginger with the sugar syrup.
4. Add the gin, lemon juice and vermouth, shake well over ice and strain into a chilled coupe glass.
5. Lean the rolled cucumber inside the glass to serve.

SPICY LYCHEE

MAKES 1

3 slices of fresh red chilli
½ thumb-sized piece of ginger, peeled and sliced (or 10ml ginger syrup if you have it)
40ml chilli-infused tequila (we use La Chica or you can make your own – see page 170)
25ml cranberry juice
25ml lime juice
20ml hibiscus syrup (page 172)
20ml lychee liqueur (we use Gabriel Boudier)
ice cubes, for shaking and serving

TO GARNISH:
1 dehydrated lime slice (page 171)

A great cocktail for an apéritif but also to pair with spicy dishes like our cod with orzo, 'nduja, confit tomato and shellfish on page 108, mussels pil pil on page 114 or our chicken and chorizo pie on page 140.

1. In the base of a cocktail shaker, muddle the sliced chilli with the ginger (or ginger syrup if using).
2. Add all the liquids to the shaker, shake well over ice and strain into a chilled coupe glass.
3. Garnish with a slice of dehydrated lime.

SAGE ADVICE

MAKES 1

8 cardamom pods
6–8 fresh sage leaves
15ml sugar syrup (page 172)
50ml Bulleit Rye whiskey
50ml freshly squeezed orange juice
25ml lemon juice
ice cubes, for shaking
1 large ice ball or cube, to serve

TO GARNISH:
1 sprig of fresh sage

With its spicy notes from the rye whiskey and earthy herbal backdrop, this is a well-balanced cocktail for matching with savoury dishes, especially any that you might like to garnish with crispy sage (see page 206), such as the butternut squash risotto starter on page 50.

1. In the base of a cocktail shaker, crush the cardamom pods and muddle the sage leaves with the sugar syrup.
2. Add the whiskey, orange juice and lemon juice, shake everything well over ice and strain into a tumbler glass over a large ice ball, if you have the mould for one, or the best, biggest ice cube you have.
3. Garnish with a sprig of fresh sage.

BLUE BLOOD BRAMBLE

MAKES 1

40ml Gordon's Mediterranean Orange Gin
25ml lemon juice
15ml blueberry syrup (page 172)
10ml crème de mûre liqueur
ice cubes, for shaking and serving

TO GARNISH:
1 orange slice
3–4 fresh blueberries
1 sprig of fresh mint

Our twist on a classic bramble cocktail adds blueberries to the simple syrup.

1. Add all the liquids to a cocktail shaker, shake well over ice and strain into a tumbler over ice.
2. Garnish with a slice of orange, fresh blueberries and a sprig of mint.

KOOL AND KURIOUS

MAKES 1

40ml Hendrick's Gin
20ml elderflower liqueur (we use St Germain)
25ml watermelon syrup (page 172)
25ml lime juice
15ml egg whites
ice cubes, for shaking

TO GARNISH:
1 cucumber slice or
1 dehydrated lime slice (page 171)
1 sprig of fresh mint

This prettiest of cocktails is a lovely option to serve with spicy dishes like our mussels pil pil on page 114. It complements the freshness of the mussels while balancing the heat from the sauce.

1. Add all the liquids to a cocktail shaker and shake well over ice. Strain and shake again without the ice to create a foam. Pour into a coupe glass or tumbler.
2. Garnish with a cucumber slice or dehydrated lime slice and a sprig of mint. The lime works well in a coupe or tumbler, while the cucumber is better in the tumbler.

KEW GARDEN

MAKES 1

2 slices of cucumber
25ml sugar syrup (page 172)
40ml Ketel One Botanicals Cucumber & Mint Vodka (or infuse your own vodka – see page 170)
25ml lime juice
ice cubes, for shaking and serving
elderflower tonic, for topping up

TO GARNISH:
1 cucumber slice
1 sprig of fresh mint

This is a favourite from the low-ABV section on our cocktail list and makes a refreshing apéritif, maybe with some oysters (page 42) or crab on toast (page 30).

1. In the base of a cocktail shaker, muddle the cucumber with the sugar syrup.
2. Add the vodka and lime juice, shake well over ice and strain into a large wine glass over cubed ice garnished with a sprig of mint.
3. Top up with elderflower tonic and finish with an extra slice of cucumber and a sprig of mint.

IT'S SUNNY SOMEWHERE

MAKES 1

40ml grapefruit-infused istil38 Pot Still Vodka
25ml lime juice
15ml rosemary sugar syrup (page 172)
ice cubes, for shaking and serving
a splash of grapefruit and rosemary tonic

TO GARNISH:
1 slice of grapefruit
1 sprig of rosemary

Bright in flavours and light in alcohol, this sunny cocktail is another favourite from our low-ABV cocktail section and works well with our Sunday roast chicken on page 128.

1. Shake the vodka, juice and syrup over ice and strain into a large wine glass with lots of ice.
2. Top up with a generous splash of grapefruit and rosemary tonic and garnish with a slice of grapefruit and a sprig of rosemary.

BLOODY MARY

MAKES 1

100ml tomato juice
50ml vodka (or tequila, for a Bloody Maria)
25ml lemon juice
ice cubes, for shaking and serving
a good dash of Worcestershire sauce
a good dash of Tabasco sauce
a good dash of Buffalo sauce
a small pinch of celery salt
a small pinch of freshly ground black pepper

TO GARNISH:
2–3 green olives
1 celery stick
1 slice of lemon

If Sunday lunch is coming hot on the heels of Saturday night, a well-made Bloody Mary (or Bloody Maria, with tequila in place of the vodka) might be just what you need while prepping the Sunday roast. We serve ours with a cool celery stalk and green olives to balance the spice from the Tabasco and Buffalo sauce.

1. Pour the tomato juice, vodka (or tequila) and lemon juice into a Boston cocktail shaker or pint glass over plenty of ice. Season with a dash or two of Worcestershire sauce, Tabasco and Buffalo sauce and a pinch of celery salt and pepper.
2. Pour into another pint glass (or the other half of the Boston shaker, if using) and then back again. Repeat four times.
3. Taste with a straw to check spice levels and adjust if needed, then strain into a tall glass over fresh ice. Add olives, a celery stick and a lemon slice.
4. Serve with the bottles of Worcestershire sauce and Tabasco on the side.

VARIATION If you want to make a jug or pitcher of Bloody Mary, just multiply the ingredients as required and stir it well over ice to chill down.

OLD-FASHIONED

MAKES 1

ice cubes, for shaking and serving
50ml bourbon
15ml sugar syrup (page 172)
2 dashes of aromatic bitters
a splash of water

TO GARNISH:
1 orange twist or slice
1 maraschino cherry (optional)

An Old-fashioned makes an excellent pre- or post-dinner cocktail but also pairs well with beef dishes like our rib-eye with béarnaise on page 94.

1. Put a large ice cube in a tumbler.
2. Fill a cocktail shaker with ice, then add the bourbon, sugar syrup, bitters and a splash of water. Stir well and strain into the rocks glass.
3. Garnish with the orange and the cherry (if using).

CUCUMBER COLLINS

MAKES 1

2 slices of cucumber
50ml Seedlip Garden 108
ice cubes, to serve
125ml soda water
25ml lime juice
25ml sugar syrup (page 172)

TO GARNISH:
1 slice of cucumber
1 sprig of fresh mint

This lovely non-alcoholic option works well with spicy dishes like our mussels pil pil on page 114, complementing the freshness of the mussels while balancing the heat from the pil pil sauce. This is a good option to batch up in a jug for a crowd – or for a boozy Collins, simply use your favourite gin instead.

1   In the base of a cocktail shaker, muddle the slices of cucumber with the Seedlip Garden 108. Strain into a tall glass over plenty of ice. Add the soda water, lime juice and sugar syrup and stir well.
2   Garnish with a cucumber slice and a sprig of fresh mint.

PLAY SAFE

MAKES 1

40ml Gordon's Alcohol Free 0.0% Gin, vanilla-infused (page 170)
25ml passionfruit purée (page 173)
25ml pineapple juice
20ml lime juice
10ml vanilla syrup, homemade (page 172) or a good brand like Monin
ice cubes, for shaking and chilling
a splash of non-alcoholic sparkling wine (look for Hollow Leg or Nozeco)

TO GARNISH:
1 dehydrated lime slice (page 171)

This is our alcohol-free take on a Porn Star Martini. It's a fun pairing for the rich scallops and brisket starter on page 40.

1   Shake the gin, purée, juices and syrup over ice and strain into a chilled coupe glass.
2   Top up with a splash of non-alcoholic sparkling wine and garnish with a dehydrated lime slice.

AMARETTO SOUR

MAKES 1

50ml Disaronno Amaretto
30ml lemon juice
15ml egg white
10ml maraschino cherry syrup
a dash of aromatic bitters
ice cubes, for shaking and serving

TO GARNISH:
1 orange twist

With its sweet and sour notes, this versatile cocktail is great as an apéritif and works well with desserts like our yogurt panna cotta with blood orange jelly and ginger crumb on page 161 – or at pretty much any other time too.

1. Add all the liquids to a cocktail shaker and shake well over ice. Strain and shake again without the ice to create a foam.
2. Pour into a tumbler over ice and garnish with an orange twist.

BANANA MAI TAI

MAKES 1

40ml banana rum, shop-bought or home-infused (see page 170)
20ml lime juice
10ml white chocolate liqueur (we use Mozart)
10ml Cointreau
10ml orgeat almond syrup
ice cubes, for shaking and serving

TO GARNISH:
dried banana chips

Though not a sweet dessert-style cocktail, this is a great match for desserts like our sticky toffee pudding on page 156, with lots of fresh acidity to cut the richness of the pudding.

1. Shake the rum, lime juice, liqueurs and syrup well over ice and strain into a tumbler glass over ice.
2. Garnish with dried banana chips.

ONE FOR THE ROAD

MAKES 1

80ml strong coffee or espresso, fully cooled
40ml West Cork Bourbon Cask Whiskey
20ml Frangelico hazelnut liqueur
20ml salted caramel syrup (page 172)
ice cubes, for stirring

TO GARNISH:
lightly whipped cream

Lots of our regulars have a dessert cocktail in place of dessert, and this twist on an Irish coffee is a top choice. Be sure to use fully cooled coffee, as any heat will over-dilute the ice.

1. Stir everything over ice in a mixing jug, pour into an Irish coffee glass and top with lightly whipped cream.

VARIATION We batch our coffee with 1kg of ground coffee to 1 litre of water, then dilute it using 7 parts coffee to 1 part Guinness for extra richness. You could do the same with cold espresso mixed in a 7:1 ratio with Guinness.

PANTRY

SAUCES
BÉARNAISE

MAKES ABOUT 120ML

100g salted butter
1 small shallot, finely diced
4 tablespoons good-quality white wine vinegar (we use Forvm Chardonnay vinegar)
2 egg yolks
a pinch of sea salt
1 teaspoon chopped fresh tarragon
a squeeze of lemon (about 1 tablespoon)

Besides being the most decadent topping for a steak (page 94), the techniques involved in making a béarnaise are worth mastering so you can also make its tarragon-free version, hollandaise, to wow brunch guests with homemade eggs Benedict (with poached eggs and ham) or eggs Florentine (with spinach).

1. To clarify the butter, gently melt it in a heavy-based saucepan over a low heat, skimming off any foam that rises to the top. Remove the pan from the heat and allow the milky layer to settle on the base of the pan, then pour off the clear fat from the top and discard the milky solids. Keep the clarified butter warm.

2. Combine the shallot with the white wine vinegar in a small saucepan. Bring to a boil, then lower the heat and simmer for 2 minutes to infuse. Remove from the heat, pass through a fine mesh sieve and discard the shallot.

3. Bring a saucepan of water to a gentle simmer. In a metal mixing bowl, whisk the egg yolks with 3 tablespoons of the vinegar reduction and a pinch of salt. Put the bowl over the saucepan of lightly simmering water, making sure the water doesn't touch the bottom of the bowl. Whisk continuously for about 5 minutes, until the colour lightens and the mixture thickens. You need to keep whisking the mixture and moving it on and off the heat periodically to prevent it from scrambling. If it's becoming too thick, add a drop of water to loosen it and prevent it from splitting.

4. Remove the pan from the heat and slowly drizzle in the melted clarified butter, whisking continuously. Taste the sauce and adjust the seasoning, then add the tarragon and a squeeze of lemon juice.

5. This is best served immediately, but if you need to hold it until other elements of the dish are ready, you can set it aside in a container at room temperature with a layer of cling film pressed directly on the surface to prevent a skin from forming. Don't keep it in a fridge or cold room, as you need to keep it a pouring consistency.

BÉCHAMEL

MAKES ABOUT 500ML

500ml full-fat milk
1 onion, halved
1 bay leaf
2 cloves
50g salted butter
50g plain flour
sea salt and ground white pepper

A good béchamel (or white sauce) is a versatile base sauce – and is one of the five mother sauces in classical cuisine. You can add other ingredients for flavour, colour or texture, such as folding in chopped fresh parsley at the end to make a parsley sauce (some like to sharpen this with a little mustard and/or lemon juice) or adding grated cheese, like we do for our 36-hour slow-braised short rib lasagne on page 98.

1. Put the milk, onion, bay leaf and cloves in a medium-sized saucepan and bring to a boil, then immediately remove the pan from the heat and set aside to infuse for 20 minutes.
2. In a separate medium-sized saucepan, melt the butter over a low heat. When the butter starts to foam, add the flour and cook for 5 minutes, stirring continuously to form a roux (paste).
3. Remove the onion, bay and cloves from the milk with a slotted spoon and discard. Gradually pour the hot milk into the roux, stirring constantly for another 7–8 minutes to thicken into a smooth sauce. Season to taste.
4. If you need to hold the sauce until other elements of the dish are ready, set it aside in a container at room temperature with a layer of cling film pressed directly on the surface to prevent a skin from forming.

HOMEMADE MAYONNAISE

MAKES ABOUT 400ML

3 egg yolks
1 tablespoon white wine vinegar
1 tablespoon Dijon mustard
sea salt and ground white pepper
300ml cold-pressed rapeseed oil or light sunflower oil

Making your own mayonnaise is simpler than you might think and gives you an excellent vehicle for all sorts of added flavours, from roast garlic or chipotle chillies to truffle oil or lobster bisque. For a truffle mayonnaise, add 2 tablespoons of truffle oil to 100ml of mayonnaise and sharpen with a little lemon juice. For a lobster mayonnaise, add 50ml of lobster bisque (page 197) to 200g mayonnaise, sharpen with a squeeze of lemon juice and season to taste with salt.

1. Put the egg yolks, vinegar, mustard and a pinch of salt and ground white pepper in a blender or food processor and blitz for 30 seconds to combine.
2. With the motor still running, start adding the oil very slowly until it emulsifies into a thick mayonnaise consistency. To avoid the mayonnaise splitting, add the oil literally one drop at a time at the very start and allow it to become incorporated before you add the next drop, though once it starts to thicken you can add the oil in a slow drizzle.
3. Refrigerate for up to three days.

TARTAR SAUCE

MAKES ABOUT 700ML

3 egg yolks
2 tablespoons white wine vinegar
1 tablespoon Dijon mustard
500ml cold-pressed rapeseed oil or light sunflower oil
100g capers, roughly chopped
100g gherkins, chopped
20g fresh parsley leaves, roughly chopped
20g fresh tarragon leaves, roughly chopped
1 shallot, finely chopped
zest of 1 lemon

A classic pairing for fish 'n' chips (page 112). You could cheat and use a good shop-bought mayonnaise for the base, then add the capers, gherkins, herbs, shallot and lemon zest.

1. Combine the egg yolks, vinegar and mustard in a blender and blitz until smooth. Keep it running on a medium speed and slowly drizzle in the oil one drop at a time to emulsify.
2. Pour into a clean bowl and fold in the chopped capers, gherkins, herbs, shallot and lemon zest.
3. Refrigerate for up to three days.

HOMEMADE BROWN SAUCE

MAKES ABOUT 500ML

250g pitted dates, finely chopped
2 Granny Smith apples
¼ teaspoon ground allspice
¼ teaspoon ground ginger
¼ nutmeg, finely grated, or ¼ teaspoon ground nutmeg (but fresh is best)
200g light brown sugar
150ml Cabernet Sauvignon vinegar (or the best red wine vinegar you can find)
150ml red wine vinegar

We serve our brown sauce with our ham hock croquettes (page 56) but many people swear by it with a full Irish fry. We like to use two different types of vinegar to layer up the flavours, so we elevate a standard red wine vinegar with single-varietal Cabernet Sauvignon vinegar for this sauce.

1. Put the finely chopped dates in a heatproof bowl. Peel the apples and grate them into the bowl, discarding the core. Mix in the spices and set aside.
2. Combine the sugar and vinegars in a small to medium-sized saucepan and bring to a boil, stirring to dissolve the sugar fully. Pour this liquid over the dates and cover the bowl with cling film. Leave for about 30 minutes to allow the dates to soak up the liquid and soften.
3. Scrape the mixture into a heavy-based saucepan and cook over a low heat for about 1½ hours, until it forms a pulp. Transfer to a blender and blitz until smooth, then pass through a fine mesh sieve and allow to cool fully.
4. Transfer to a sterilised jar (page 26), seal and store in a cool, dark place for up to two months. Once opened, keep it in the fridge and use within a week.

TZATZIKI

MAKES ABOUT 600ML

500g Greek-style yogurt
½ large cucumber
2 garlic cloves, minced
zest of 1 lemon
1 sprig of fresh coriander, stalks and leaves finely chopped
1 sprig of fresh thyme, leaves picked and finely chopped
a few sprigs of fresh mint, leaves picked and finely chopped
2 tablespoons good-quality extra-virgin olive oil
1 tablespoon honey
a pinch of sea salt

Fresh and zingy, this Greek condiment is easy to whip up and is useful with Mediterranean, Middle Eastern and even Indian curry flavours. Straining the yogurt give this a thick consistency but you could skip this step for a looser result.

1. Put the yogurt in a clean cheesecloth or muslin cloth, then put it in a colander set over a bowl and leave in the fridge overnight to strain.
2. Grate the cucumber down as far as the seeds on all sides. Put in a clean cloth and squeeze out all the water until you are left with a dry pulp. Mix this into the strained yogurt with all the other ingredients and refrigerate until needed or for up to four days.

STOCKS, JUS AND GRAVY
PRAWN STOCK

MAKES 2 LITRES

3kg prawn shells
2 tablespoons neutral oil
75g salted butter
2 onions, roughly chopped
2 carrots, roughly chopped
2 leeks, roughly chopped
2 celery sticks, roughly chopped
1 fennel bulb, roughly chopped
2 bay leaves
a large handful of fresh parsley
20 black peppercorns
100ml brandy
2 tablespoons tomato purée
200ml white wine
6 litres cold water

We use this stock for cooking orzo or risotto, in fish sauces and soups, and as the base for our prawn bisque (see below).

1 Preheat the oven to 190°C.
2 Put the prawn shells on a baking tray and roast in the preheated oven for about 35 minutes, until golden brown.
3 Meanwhile, heat the oil in a large heavy-based saucepan over a medium-high heat. Add the butter and allow it to melt. When it starts to foam, add the vegetables, bay leaves, parsley and peppercorns and cook for about 5 minutes, until golden, stirring to brown them evenly.
4 Add the brandy and flambé by using a long match or chef's lighter to set the brandy alight in the pan and allowing the flame to burn off the alcohol. Add the tomato purée and cook for 3–4 minutes. Deglaze the pan with the white wine, stirring until the bottom of the pot comes clean, then reduce the liquid by half.
5 Add the roasted prawn shells and cold water, bring to a simmer and cook, uncovered, for 2–3 hours, until it has reduced right down to about 2 litres of liquid, periodically skimming any scum or impurities that come to the surface.
6 Strain through a fine mesh sieve, cool and refrigerate for up to four days. This stock also freezes well for up to three months (see page 25).

PRAWN BISQUE

MAKES ABOUT 1.5 LITRES

150g salted butter
1 onion, peeled and chopped
1 carrot, peeled and chopped
1 celery stick, chopped
1 leek, chopped
1 garlic clove, bashed
8 fennel seeds
1 bay leaf
50ml brandy
50g tomato purée
200ml white wine
2 litres prawn stock (see above)
100ml cream

You can use this bisque as a soup or sauce that will complement most fish or to build flavour in dishes like the cod with orzo, 'nduja, confit tomato and shellfish on page 108. The prawn stock itself freezes well (make it in advance and finish as below) and the bisque freezes well too.

1 Melt the butter in a heavy-based saucepan over a medium-high heat. When the butter starts to foam, add the vegetables, garlic, fennel seeds and bay leaf and cook for about 5 minutes, until golden, stirring to brown them evenly.
2 Add the brandy and flambé by using a long match or chef's lighter to set the brandy alight in the pan and allowing the flame to burn off the alcohol. Add the tomato purée and cook for 3–4 minutes. Deglaze the pan with the white wine, stirring until the bottom of the pot comes clean. Add the stock and reduce by half.
3 Pass through a fine mesh sieve, then pour the strained stock back into the pan and add the cream. Reduce until it reaches a light soup consistency.
4 Strain through a fine mesh sieve, cool and refrigerate for up to four days.

LOBSTER BISQUE

MAKES ABOUT 700ML

1–2 tablespoons neutral oil
1 whole lobster shell
1 large banana shallot, quartered
1 carrot, roughly chopped
4 garlic cloves, bashed
1 lemongrass stalk
1 bay leaf
1 star anise
20 pink peppercorns
250g tomato purée
200ml brandy
1 litre chicken stock (page 199)

As with the prawn bisque on the previous page, you can use this as a soup or sauce, especially with Asian fish dishes, and in dishes like our arancini (page 33) with lobster mayonnaise (page 193).

1. Heat a little oil in a large heavy-based saucepan over a high heat. Add the lobster shell, shallot, carrot and garlic. Bash the lemongrass with the side of a chef's knife to release its flavour, then add it to the pan with the bay leaf, star anise and peppercorns. Roast off everything for 5–6 minutes, stirring, until the veg start to caramelise and turn a rich golden brown.
2. Add the tomato purée, reduce the heat slightly and cook for a further 5 minutes, stirring regularly. Turn the heat back up for the last minute or so.
3. With the heat high, add the brandy and flambé by using a long match or chef's lighter to set the brandy alight in the pan and allowing the flame to burn off the alcohol. Let it burn out, then when the flame drops you can stir it again before adding the chicken stock. Bring to a boil, reduce the heat to a simmer and cook gently for 30 minutes.
4. Strain through a fine mesh sieve, cool and refrigerate for up to four days.

RED WINE JUS

MAKES ABOUT 600ML

20g salted butter
1 tablespoon neutral oil
2 shallots, quartered
2 carrots, roughly chopped
1 celery stick, roughly chopped
1 garlic clove, roughly chopped
1 bay leaf
a few sprigs of fresh thyme
a small handful of fresh parsley
20g tomato purée
500ml red wine
1 tablespoon caster sugar
1 tablespoon balsamic vinegar
2 litres beef stock (page 199)

Just a little red wine jus adds richness and depth of flavour to all sorts of dishes, from mussels pil pil (page 114) to a Sunday roast gravy (page 200), so consider freezing it into ice cubes for ease of use (see page 25).

1. Heat the butter and oil in a heavy-based saucepan over a medium heat. Add the vegetables, garlic and herbs and cook for about 5 minutes, until the veg develop a nice golden brown colour.
2. Stir in the tomato purée and cook for a minute or two. Add the wine, sugar and balsamic, bring up to a simmer and reduce by half. Add the beef stock and reduce slowly for about 35 minutes, until it reaches a sauce consistency.
3. Pass through a fine mesh sieve and allow to cool. This will keep in the fridge for up to five days and freezes well for up to three months (see page 25).

PORT JUS

MAKES ABOUT 600ML

20g salted butter
1 tablespoon neutral oil
2 shallots, peeled and quartered
2 carrots, roughly chopped
1 celery stick, chopped
2 garlic cloves, bashed
10 black peppercorns
6 juniper berries
1 bay leaf
1 sprig of fresh thyme
1 sprig of fresh parsley
20g tomato purée
500ml port
1 tablespoon caster sugar
1 tablespoon balsamic vinegar
2 litres venison stock or beef stock (page 199)

This port jus is used in our venison dish on page 104. It makes more than you will need but it freezes well (see page 25) or you could halve the ingredients to make about 300ml.

1. Heat the butter and oil in a heavy-based saucepan over a medium-high heat. Add the vegetables, garlic, spices and herbs and cook for about 5 minutes, until the veg develop a nice golden brown colour.
2. Stir in the tomato purée and cook for a minute or two. Add the port, sugar and balsamic, bring up to a simmer and reduce by half. Add the stock and reduce slowly for about 35 minutes, until it reaches a sauce consistency.
3. Pass through a fine mesh sieve and allow to cool. This will keep in the fridge for up to five days and freezes well for up to three months (see page 25).

CIDER JUS

MAKES ABOUT 350ML

1 tablespoon neutral oil
1 banana shallot, chopped
1 celery stick, chopped
1 garlic clove, bashed
1 sprig of fresh thyme
1 bay leaf
500ml dry cider
200ml red wine jus (page 197)

Combining the richness of our red wine jus with the lip-smacking tang of a dry cider, this cider jus is magic with our pork chops with colcannon, black pudding and apple purée on page 106.

1. Heat the oil in a saucepan over a medium-high heat. Add the shallot, celery, garlic, thyme and bay leaf and cook for 5–6 minutes to colour and caramelise. Add the cider and reduce by half, then add the red wine jus and reduce by a quarter.
2. Strain through a fine mesh sieve. This will keep in the fridge for up to five days and freezes well for up to three months (see page 25).

CHICKEN STOCK

MAKES ABOUT 1.5 LITRES

4 raw chicken carcasses (ask your butcher for these)
4 litres water
2 onions, roughly chopped
2 carrots, roughly chopped
2 celery sticks, roughly chopped
1 leek, roughly chopped
2 bay leaves
1 sprig of fresh parsley
1 sprig of fresh thyme
5 black peppercorns
3 white peppercorns

This is a clear chicken stock made with raw carcasses as opposed to one made with leftover roast chicken bones. Ask your butchers for the carcasses.

1. Put everything in a large stockpot and bring to a boil, then reduce the heat to low and simmer gently for 4 hours, uncovered, periodically skimming off any scum or impurities that rise to the top.
2. Cool, strain through a fine mesh sieve and refrigerate for up to five days. This will also freeze well for up to three months (see page 25).

BEEF STOCK

MAKES ABOUT 2 LITRES

3kg beef or veal bones (ask your butcher for these)
40g salted butter
20ml neutral oil
2 large onions, unpeeled and chopped
4 carrots, roughly chopped
2 leeks, roughly chopped
1 whole garlic bulb, halved horizontally
3 bay leaves
a large handful of fresh thyme sprigs
a large handful of fresh parsley
5 black peppercorns
9 litres cold water

You'll need a very large stockpot for this recipe so that you can add such a large volume of water and you'll also need lots of time to let it bubble away – but we promise it'll be worth it. You can use the same method to make a venison stock, which we use for our port jus (see opposite) to pair with the venison main course on page 104.

1. Preheat the oven to 220°C.
2. Put the bones on a roasting tray and roast in the preheated oven for 1 hour, until dark brown.
3. Heat the butter and oil in a very large heavy-based stockpot over a medium-high heat. Add all the vegetables, garlic, herbs and peppercorns and cook for 6–8 minutes, until the vegetables are a rich, dark caramelised colour, stirring regularly to brown everything evenly.
4. Add the bones to the pot, discarding any fat from the tray. Pour in the water and bring to a boil, then reduce the heat and simmer gently for 7–8 hours, periodically skimming off any scum or impurities that come to the top.
5. Cool, strain through a fine mesh sieve and refrigerate for up to five days. This will also freeze well for up to three months (see page 25).

SUNDAY ROAST GRAVY

MAKES ABOUT 500ML

1 tablespoon neutral oil
1 banana shallot, diced
1 bay leaf
1 sprig of fresh thyme
500ml chicken stock (page 199)
100ml red wine jus (page 197)
roasting juices from the roast chicken (page 128) or beef (page 130)
30g salted butter, chilled and diced
sea salt and freshly ground black pepper

We use a mixture of chicken stock and red wine jus as the basis of our gravy, then incorporate the roasting pan juices from the chicken or beef and finish with some butter for a glossy shine.

1   Heat the oil in a saucepan over a medium heat. Add the shallot, bay leaf and thyme and cook for about 4 minutes, until golden.
2   Add the chicken stock and jus and bring up to a simmer, then add the roasting juices from the chicken or beef. Simmer for a few more minutes, until it reaches the desired gravy consistency.
3   Take the pan off the heat. Add the cold butter one cube at a time, whisking until emulsified. Season and pass through a fine mesh sieve before serving hot. This will keep well in the fridge for up to five days and will freeze well for up to three months (see page 25).

PASTRY, PASTA, POTATO
SUET PASTRY

MAKES ABOUT 700G (ENOUGH FOR 1 LARGE PIE)

500g self-raising flour
1 teaspoon (5g) baking powder
100g beef suet, shredded
100g cold salted butter, diced
4 egg yolks, beaten
a pinch of sea salt
1–2 tablespoons cold water

This traditional pastry has a savoury flavour that works well with meaty pies, like our beef and Guinness pie on page 142 or the lamb hotpot on page 86.

1. Sift the flour and baking powder together into a large bowl, then make a well in the centre and add the suet, butter, egg yolks and salt. Mix well to combine, then add a little cold water, bit by bit, to bring it all together into a smooth dough. Use a flat-bladed knife to start mixing the suet, eggs and butter into the flour, then use your hands once you start adding the water to bring it all together.
2. Wrap well in cling film and refrigerate for at least 30 minutes, then roll it out on a floured surface to the shape and size of your serving dish.

HOMEMADE PASTA

MAKES ABOUT 700G

500g '00' flour, plus extra if needed
3 eggs
6 egg yolks
1 teaspoon olive oil
a pinch of sea salt

While fresh pasta has become a lot more accessible to buy than when our head chef, Mark, first fell in love with it as a budding teenage cook, it's still worth investing in a pasta machine to make your own fresh pasta on a whim. It also opens up possibilities like the ravioli on page 46.

1. Put the flour, eggs and egg yolks in a food processor and mix until the dough begins to form a ball. Add the olive oil and a pinch of salt and blend again to incorporate.
2. Lightly flour a clean work surface. Tip the dough out of the food processor and knead by hand for about 5 minutes, until smooth, adding a little more flour if it starts to stick. Cover tightly with cling film and refrigerate for 1–2 hours.
3. Set a pasta machine to the thickest setting. Feed the pasta through the rollers three to four times on each setting until you get to the thinnest one, lightly dusting the pasta sheet with flour if required. Passing the pasta through the rollers multiple times on each setting removes any lines or graininess in the pasta and ensures a thinner, silkier texture.
4. Once you've prepared your pasta, covering it with a damp cloth will help prevent it from drying out while you're constructing the dish. Alternatively, if not using your pasta straight away, you could blanch it and refrigerate until ready to use or hang it up to dry.
5. When ready to use, cut the pasta sheets as needed.

BASIC GNOCCHI

MAKES 1KG COOKED GNOCCHI

500kg floury potatoes (we use Roosters), scrubbed

175g '00' flour, plus extra if needed

50g Parmesan cheese, finely grated

2 level teaspoons (12g) fine sea salt, plus extra for the baking tray

1 egg

1 egg yolk

As with our homemade pasta on the previous page, it's worth mastering how to make your own gnocchi, not least so you can experiment with adding different flavourings to the base recipe. For example, to make a cep gnocchi, simply add 30g cep powder to the dough along with the flour. Once you have cut the gnocchi into even-sized pillows, you can roll these into balls and press the centre to give a mushroom-like shape – see page 116 for a serving suggestion.

1. Preheat the oven to 180°C.
2. Cover a baking tray with an even layer of salt (fine or coarse will do; it's there to extract and absorb moisture from the potatoes). Put the potatoes on top and spike the top of each one with a fork. Bake in the preheated oven for about 90 minutes, until a knife will go through them easily.
3. Sift the flour into a large mixing bowl, then add the Parmesan and 2 teaspoons of salt. Mix to combine, then make a well in the centre. Beat the egg and egg yolk together in a small bowl and add this to the well.
4. Remove the potatoes from the oven and cut them in half. Scoop the flesh into a mouli or ricer or push it through a fine mesh sieve into the mixing bowl.
5. Lightly flour your hands and mix everything together with your fingers to incorporate and knead together to form a smooth, soft dough, adding a little more flour if needed to keep it quite dry.
6. Flour a clean surface. Tip the dough out onto the countertop and cut it into six even balls. Working quickly and with a light touch, roll each ball into a long sausage shape about 2.5cm wide, then cut the sausage shape into even, bite-sized pillows.
7. Bring a large pot of salted water to a boil. Add the gnocchi and blanch just until they float to the top, about 3 minutes. Drain well.
8. Use immediately or immerse in iced water to cool them quickly, then drain well, spread them out on a baking tray lined with greaseproof paper, cover and refrigerate for up to three days.

BAKED POTATO MASH

MAKES ABOUT 1KG

4 large floury baking potatoes (about 1kg; we use Roosters), scrubbed
100ml milk
100ml cream
2 tablespoons cold salted butter
2 teaspoons sea salt, plus extra for the baking tray
¼ teaspoon ground white pepper

This is a great way of making mashed potatoes, as the potatoes bake in their own steam. You can use this baked potato mash as a side for all sorts of dishes or as a topping for our luxe shepherd's pie (page 146) or fish pie (page 148), enriched with egg yolks at the last minute for a glossy topping.

To make colcannon, cook the recipe as below, but when the potatoes are ready and while you're heating the cream and milk, blanch 250g finely sliced Savoy cabbage in boiling salted water for about 3 minutes, until tender, and drain well. Pass the potatoes into the cream, then add the blanched cabbage together with a bunch of thinly sliced spring onions and eight thinly sliced fresh sage leaves. Season to taste with salt and white pepper.

You can reserve the baked potato skins and use them to make loaded skins. Just deep-fry (see page 25) and season well, then load up with grated cheese, crispy bacon lardons, thinly sliced red onion and garlic mayo.

1. Preheat the oven to 180°C.
2. Cover a baking tray with an even layer of salt (fine or coarse will do; it's there to extract and absorb moisture from the potatoes). Put the potatoes on top and spike the top of each one with a fork. Bake in the preheated oven for about 90 minutes, until a knife will go through them easily.
3. When the potatoes are ready, heat the milk and cream in a large saucepan.
4. Remove the potatoes from the oven and cut them in half. Scoop the flesh into a mouli or ricer or push it through a fine mesh sieve directly into the hot cream mixture in the pan. Fold together with a spatula. Once it's fairly smooth, fold in the cold butter and continue stirring until silky smooth. Season with the salt and white pepper.
5. This will keep well for up to three days in the fridge.

PICKLES
PICKLED CARROT AND CELERIAC

80g caster sugar
200ml white wine vinegar
50ml water
1 large carrot, diced into even 2cm square cubes
100g celeriac, diced into even 2cm square cubes

This quick and easy pickle tastes best on its first or second day, though it will keep in the fridge for up to a week. It makes enough to serve with the scallops and brisket starter on page 40 but you can multiply the quantities to make a bigger batch.

1. Combine the sugar, vinegar and water in a saucepan and heat until the sugar dissolves. Remove the pan from the heat and set aside.
2. In a separate small saucepan, blanch the diced vegetables in boiling salted water for 2 minutes, then plunge straight into iced water to arrest the cooking process. Strain and add to the warm pickle brine. Set aside to cool.
3. Serve at room temperature with the scallop starter or transfer to a sterilised jar (see page 26) and keep in the fridge for up to a week.

PICKLED RHUBARB

200g caster sugar
140ml Chardonnay vinegar
35ml water
1 bay leaf
1 teaspoon sea salt
4 sticks of champagne rhubarb, cut into pieces 4cm long

We serve this with our pig's head fritter on page 59 but it can be used with any rich meat or fish. It would be excellent with smoked mackerel.

1. Put everything except the rhubarb in a small saucepan and bring to a boil. Put the rhubarb in a heatproof bowl, pour over the hot pickling liquid and cover for 30 minutes. Alternatively, you can do this in a vacuum-sealed bag in a water bath at 80°C for 15 minutes.
2. Serve at room temperature with the pig's head fritter or transfer to a sterilised jar (see page 26) and keep in the fridge for up to a week.

PICKLED CHILLIES

MAKES ABOUT 20G

100g caster sugar
200ml white wine vinegar
50ml water
2–3 fresh red chillies, sliced

We use these quick pickled chillies with our side of charred broccoli on page 122. They would also be good in stir-fries and noodles.

1. Combine the sugar, vinegar and water in a small saucepan and heat until the sugar dissolves. Remove the pan from the heat, add the sliced chillies and set aside to cool.
2. Serve at room temperature with the charred broccoli or transfer to a sterilised jar (see page 26) and keep in the fridge for up to a week.

CUCUMBER PICKLE

SERVES 4-5

1 cucumber
50g caster sugar
150ml water
100ml Chardonnay vinegar (or regular white wine vinegar)
1 small bunch of fresh dill, leaves picked and finely chopped

This quick pickle is best used on the day it's made but you could strain the pickling liquid and reuse it for another batch.

1. Thinly slice the cucumber with a mandolin or peel into ribbons.
2. Bring the sugar, water and vinegar to a boil in a small saucepan over a medium heat to dissolve the sugar. Take the pan off the heat and allow to cool. Add the cucumber and dill and allow to marinate for at least 30 minutes.
3. Serve at room temperature with the chicken liver parfait on page 60 or transfer to a sterilised jar (see page 26) and keep in the fridge in an airtight jar for up to a week.

PICKLED GIROLLE MUSHROOMS

MAKES 350G

350g girolle mushrooms
800ml water
700ml white wine vinegar
4 medium banana shallots, thinly sliced into rings
1 garlic clove, bashed
1 sprig of fresh thyme
1 blade of mace
10 black peppercorns

We use these pickled girolle mushrooms to elevate our white onion soup on page 72 but they are also an excellent garnish for vegetable risottos or to pair with venison or chicken dishes. This is a hardier pickle than the previous ones and is a great way to extend the girolle season, so consider making an extra jar (or two). You could also use this same method to pickle other mushrooms, such as shiitake, which are more widely available year round and have a more robust character. It's important to use a sterilised jar (see page 26) so your beautiful pickle doesn't spoil.

1. Put the mushrooms in a large heatproof bowl.
2. Combine all the other ingredients in a large saucepan over a medium-high heat. As soon as the liquid comes to a boil, pour it immediately over the mushrooms and cover the bowl with a lid or cling film. Leave to infuse at room temperature for 24 hours.
3. The next day, transfer the mushrooms and all of the pickling ingredients to a sterilised jar (or jars, if you don't have one that's big enough to fit all of them; see page 26) and pour in enough of the pickling liquid to cover. Seal with the lid and store in the fridge, where they will keep for several months.

GARNISHES, PURÉES, CHUTNEYS, GELS, JELLIES, FOAMS & GRANITA

CRISPY SAGE LEAVES

neutral oil, for frying
1 small bunch of fresh sage, leaves picked

This smart garnish elevates a dish while keeping things earthy and humble. The same technique can be used for other herbs, such as basil, which would need to be fried for just 10 seconds.

1. Heat the oil in a deep-fryer until it's nice and hot or add a generous layer of oil to a shallow pan.
2. Add the sage leaves and fry for 30 seconds to crisp them up, then transfer with a slotted spoon to kitchen paper to dry.
3. These will keep well in a sealed contained for up to a week.

DEEP-FRIED KALE OR CAVOLO NERO

100g kale or cavolo nero
neutral oil, for frying
a pinch of sea salt

Use as a garnish for dishes like risotto or our venison with black mushroom powder on page 104, or increase the quantities and serve as a snack.

1. Wash the kale well, remove the tough central rib and pat the leaves dry. Tear or roughly chop into bite-sized pieces.
2. Heat the oil in a deep-fryer until it's nice and hot or add a generous layer of oil to a shallow pan.
3. Add the dried leaves and fry for 10 seconds to crisp them up, then transfer with a slotted spoon to kitchen paper to dry. Season with salt to taste.
4. These will keep crisp in a sealed contained for a few days.

CONFIT TOMATOES

10 cherry tomatoes
a generous pinch of sea salt
a generous pinch of caster sugar
a generous drizzling of olive oil

The below quantities are sufficient for the cod with orzo recipe on page 108 but you could increase the quantities and store the confit tomatoes in the fridge for a few days to use in other pasta dishes or salads.

1. Slice the tomatoes in half and season generously with salt, caster sugar and a drizzle of olive oil, mixing to combine.
2. In the restaurant we confit them under the hot lights for several hours to slowly intensify their flavour, but at home you could lay them on a baking tray lined with greaseproof paper and put this on the lowest setting of your oven for 4 hours or in the hot press for 24 hours.

MUSHROOM DUXELLES

450g fresh Portobello mushrooms
100ml olive oil
50ml balsamic vinegar
2 garlic cloves, bashed
1 sprig of fresh thyme
sea salt and freshly ground black pepper
50g pine nuts, toasted
20g Parmesan cheese, roughly grated

We use this with our chicken supreme with gnocchi and peas on page 92 but it works equally well with lamb rump. Or you can use it as an alternative for the pickled girolles in the white onion soup on page 72.

1. Preheat the oven to 190°C. Put a baking tray in the oven to heat up too.
2. Peel the mushrooms and put them on the heated baking tray, then rub them all over with the olive oil and balsamic vinegar, making sure to cover all areas. Add the garlic, thyme and a generous seasoning of salt, then cover with foil. Roast in the preheated oven for about 20 minutes, until tender.
3. Spread the pine nuts out on a small baking tray and toast in the hot oven for 3–4 minutes, until they turn golden, watching carefully so they don't burn. This gives the most even results, but you can also toast them in a pan or under a hot grill, shaking regularly.
4. Put the roast mushrooms in a blender with the toasted nuts and Parmesan and pulse briefly to a rough, breadcrumb-like texture.
5. Season to taste and set aside or cover and refrigerate for up to three days.

BABA GANOUSH

MAKES ABOUT 500G, ENOUGH FOR THE LAMB RECIPE ON PAGE 103

2 tablespoons olive oil
500g aubergines, peeled and finely diced
sea salt and freshly ground black pepper
80g caster sugar
juice of 2 lemons
1 small onion, thinly sliced
1 teaspoon ras el hanout
1 teaspoon harissa

This spiced aubergine condiment is highly versatile. The harissa gives it a bright orange hue as well as fragrant heat. Serve it as a colourful picnic dip with hummus and flatbread, as part of a Middle Eastern mezze spread or with a main course like our lamb rump with Moroccan spices on page 103.

1. Heat 1 tablespoon of oil in a frying pan on a medium heat. Season the aubergines and add to the pan with the sugar and lemon juice, then cook for 6–8 minutes, until soft and lightly caramelised. Set aside.
2. Heat the remaining tablespoon of oil in a separate pan over a medium-low heat. Add the onion, season well and cook for 6–8 minutes, stirring occasionally, until soft and golden. Add the ras el hanout and the harissa and cook for about 5 minutes.
3. Transfer to a blender, add the aubergines and blitz until silky smooth. Pass through a fine mesh sieve and adjust the seasoning.
4. This will keep in the fridge for up to four days.

SQUASH OR PUMPKIN PURÉE

MAKES ABOUT 700G

150g salted butter
1 large butternut squash or 1 small pumpkin (we love to use Crown Prince), peeled, deseeded and diced
1 generous tablespoon mascarpone cheese
sea salt
a squeeze of lemon

We use squash and pumpkin purée in a number of dishes in The Old Spot. Below are two different techniques for making it. The main recipe will give a cleaner, more subtle result, while the roasting technique adds deeper flavours.

This recipe works equally well with pumpkin or any other type of squash if you'd like to play around. The mascarpone adds a subtle lactic sweetness but you could use crème fraîche for a sharper flavour. Any leftovers can be added to a soup or frozen and used later in ravioli.

1. Melt the butter in a saucepan over a medium heat. When the butter starts to foam, add the diced squash or pumpkin and reduce the heat a little. Cover the pan and cook gently for about 15 minutes, until very soft, stirring occasionally to ensure it isn't colouring.
2. Alternatively, you'll get a more robust flavour if you roast the squash or pumpkin before puréeing. Cut it in half, scoop out the seeds, drizzle with olive oil, season well and add some torn fresh sage and sprigs of thyme, then roast at 180°C for 40–60 minutes, until completely soft. Scoop out the flesh, discarding the skin, then blitz with about 50ml of chicken stock (page 199) and 1 tablespoon of mascarpone or crème fraîche, season with salt and pepper and a squeeze of lemon to sharpen.
3. Either way, put in a blender with the mascarpone and blitz until smooth. Pass through a fine mesh sieve and season with a pinch of salt and a squeeze of lemon.
4. Refrigerate for up to three days.

CELERIAC PURÉE

MAKES ABOUT 300G

a generous knob of unsalted butter
200g celeriac, peeled, trimmed and diced into small, even pieces
100ml cream
sea salt and freshly ground black pepper
a wedge of lemon

We use this purée in our scallops starter on page 40 as a foil to the pickled carrot and celeriac. It's also a great flavour to pair with mushrooms, nuts, poultry and game, such as venison.

1. Melt the butter in a large saucepan over a medium heat. When the butter starts to foam, add the celeriac, cover the pan and sweat for 5 minutes, until it starts to soften without colouring. Reduce the heat to low, then add the cream, season with salt and pepper and cook for 10 minutes, until the celeriac is completely soft.
2. Use a slotted spoon to transfer the celeriac to a blender and blitz briefly, then gradually pour in the hot cream as you blend to a smooth purée. Season with a little lemon juice to sharpen.
3. Set aside until ready to use or cover and refrigerate for up to three days.

GARLIC PURÉE

MAKES ABOUT 350G

250g garlic cloves, peeled
100ml cream
sea salt and ground white pepper

We use this punchy purée to give depth to our cep gnocchi on page 116. You could add any leftovers to soups or stews.

1. Bring a medium-sized saucepan of water to a boil. Add the peeled garlic cloves and blanch for 4 minutes, then drain and refresh in cold water. Repeat this process two more times.
2. Put the blanched garlic and cream in the saucepan and bring up to a simmer. Cook for about 10 minutes, until the cream has reduced by half. Blend and pass through a fine mesh sieve. Season with salt and white pepper, then put into a squeezy bottle. This will keep in the fridge for up to five days.

APPLE PURÉE

MAKES ABOUT 500G

4 Granny Smith apples, peeled, cored and chopped
2 tablespoons caster sugar
juice of ½ lemon
a splash of water

We serve this simple apple purée with our pork chops and black pudding on page 106.

1. Put everything in a saucepan over a medium-low heat, cover and sweat gently for 6–8 minutes, until the apples are soft.
2. Blitz with a hand blender, pass through a fine mesh sieve and set aside until ready to serve.
3. This will keep for up to five days in the fridge.

APRICOT PURÉE

MAKES ABOUT 500G

500g dried apricots
450g golden raisins
60g capers
500ml apple juice
1 teaspoon Dijon mustard

This handy purée can be used on a cheeseboard (see page 166) or with our cep gnocchi (page 116), ham hock terrine (page 57) or chicken liver parfait (page 60).

1. Put everything in a saucepan over a medium heat and bring to a boil, then reduce the heat to cook on a simmer for about 45 minutes, until it has a jammy consistency.
2. Blend until smooth and pass through a fine mesh sieve. Put into a squeezy bottle and use warm or cold.
3. This will keep in the fridge for up to five days.

RHUBARB PURÉE

MAKES ABOUT 400G

400g champagne rhubarb
150g caster sugar
juice of 1 lemon
a splash of water
a scant ¼ teaspoon xanthan gum

We use this rhubarb purée with our pig's head fritters on page 59 but it would work brilliantly with smoked mackerel too, whether to accompany a smoked mackerel pâté on thin toasts as a party snack or to dress a smoked mackerel salad.

1 Put the rhubarb in a saucepan with the sugar, lemon juice and a small splash of water. Bring to a boil, then reduce the heat and cook for about 15 minutes, until soft.
2 Put in a blender and blitz until completely smooth. Add the xanthan gum and blitz for another minute. Pass through a fine mesh sieve and refrigerate until needed or for up to five days.

PLUM CHUTNEY

MAKES ABOUT 900G

1 tablespoon neutral oil
4 banana shallots, chopped
1kg plums, stoned and quartered
400g light brown sugar
400ml apple cider vinegar
zest and juice of 1 orange
4 cloves
3 fresh bay leaves
1 cinnamon stick
½ teaspoon ground allspice
½ teaspoon ground ginger

This chutney will be delicious to eat straight away but the flavour will improve over a few weeks.

1 Heat the oil in a heavy-based pan over a medium heat. Add the shallots, cover the pan and sweat for 7–8 minutes, until soft and translucent. Add the plums, sugar, vinegar, orange zest and juice, herbs and spices and bring to a boil, then reduce the heat to low and cook, uncovered, for about 2 hours, until the liquid has evaporated, stirring occasionally so it doesn't catch.
2 Allow to cool, then spoon into sterilised jars (see page 26). Store in a cool, dark place, where it should keep for at least 12 months. Once opened, it will keep for at least a week in the fridge.

ORANGE AND GINGER GEL

MAKES ABOUT 500G

80g thin orange peel (3–4 oranges)
220ml freshly squeezed orange juice
50ml ginger syrup, shop-bought or homemade (see the intro)
4g agar-agar powder (you can buy this online)
4g sea salt

We use this with our oxtail beignet on page 53 but it also pairs well with meaty, oily or smoked fish, smoked or roast duck, or fattier cuts of pork.

You can buy ginger syrup from good food stores and supermarkets. Alternatively, you can make a simple ginger syrup by dissolving one part caster sugar in one part hot water, adding one part peeled, sliced ginger and simmering for 15 minutes, then cooling and steeping for 1 hour to infuse before straining and discarding the ginger.

1. Use a fine, sharp peeler to get a very thin peel from the oranges without any of the bitter white membranes.
2. Bring a small saucepan of water to a boil, then add the peels and blanch for just 15 seconds. Drain the water and submerge the peels completely in fresh water to cool quickly. Drain and repeat the process two more times.
3. Put the orange juice in a blender with the blanched peels, ginger syrup, agar-agar and salt, and blitz until smooth. Pour this into a saucepan and bring to a boil for 1 minute, stirring to prevent it from catching and burning. Transfer to a bowl and refrigerate to cool completely and set.
4. Once set, transfer to a blender and blitz again to a smooth gel. Spoon into a piping bag or squeezy bottle and refrigerate for up to four days.

BEETROOT GEL

MAKES ABOUT 600ML

4 medium even-sized beetroots (about 500g)
olive oil, for drizzling
50g salted butter
40g caster sugar
½ level teaspoon (3g) fine sea salt, plus extra for seasoning
1 shallot, chopped
2 sprigs of fresh thyme
200ml chicken stock (page 199) or vegetable stock
20ml white wine vinegar
a scant ¼ teaspoon xanthan gum

The xanthan gum used here helps to create a nice gel-like consistency and prevents any leakage of liquid.

1. Preheat the oven to 180°C.
2. Put the beetroot on a piece of foil, drizzle over some olive oil, season with salt and wrap up the beets as tightly as possible. Put the parcel on a baking tray and bake in the preheated oven for around 70 minutes, until the beetroot are cooked through – the tip of a sharp knife should glide in easily. Remove from the oven and carefully open up the foil – watch out for the escaping steam. Allow to cool for 5 minutes before peeling. Discard the peel and chop the beetroot.
3. Melt the butter in a frying pan together with the sugar and salt over a medium heat and caramelise for 2 minutes before adding the shallot and cooking for 4–5 minutes more, until golden. Add the beetroot and thyme and cook for 5 minutes, then deglaze the pan with the stock and white wine vinegar, stirring until the base of the pan comes clean. Allow to reduce until almost all the liquid has evaporated.
4. Remove the thyme, then transfer to a blender and blitz until smooth. Add the xanthan gum and blend for another minute. Pass through a fine mesh sieve and store in a squeezy bottle in the fridge for up to four days.

BLOODY MARY JELLY

MAKES ENOUGH FOR 2 DOZEN OYSTERS

3 gelatine leaves
200ml tomato juice
50ml vodka
1 tablespoon lemon juice
1 teaspoon Tabasco sauce
a few shakes of Worcestershire sauce
a pinch of celery salt
a pinch of freshly ground black pepper

This is one of our favourite toppings for oysters (see page 42), as are the yuzu jelly, apple foam and sake and cucumber granita below.

1. Soak the gelatine leaves in a small bowl of cold water for 5 minutes, then pour off the water.
2. Mix the remaining ingredients together in a separate bowl, then gently heat 50ml of this liquid and add the soaked gelatine leaves. Stir until the gelatine has fully melted, then add this back to the rest of the seasoned tomato juice. Place in a container and refrigerate to set, about 2 hours. Once set, finely chop into a caviar-like texture and set aside until ready to use. This will keep in the fridge for a week.

YUZU JELLY

MAKES ENOUGH FOR 2 DOZEN OYSTERS

3 gelatine leaves
250ml yuzu juice
50g caster sugar

Another topping for oysters (see page 42). We add some Goatsbridge trout caviar just before serving.

1. Soak the gelatine leaves in a small bowl of cold water for 5 minutes, then pour off the water.
2. Gently heat the yuzu juice and sugar, stirring until the sugar has dissolved. Add 50ml to the soaked and drained gelatine and stir until the gelatine has fully melted. Add this to the rest of the sweetened yuzu. Put in a container and refrigerate to set, about 2 hours. Once set, finely chop into a caviar-like texture and set aside until ready to use. This will keep in the fridge for a week.

APPLE AND MINT FOAM

MAKES ENOUGH FOR 2 DOZEN OYSTERS

250ml fresh apple juice
5 fresh mint leaves
1½ gelatine leaves
50ml cold water
50ml warm water

This uses a handy piece of kit called a cream charger, which you can find in most kitchen shops. If you don't have one, make this as a granita instead (see the sake and cucumber granita recipe opposite).

1. Blend the apple juice and mint leaves and allow to sit for 30 minutes to settle and for the flavours to infuse.
2. Soak the gelatine leaves in the cold water for 5 minutes, then transfer the gelatine to the warm water and stir until fully melted. Add this to the minty apple juice and refrigerate for about 2 hours to set.
3. When ready to use, pour into a cream charger to create a foam. Alternatively, freeze as per the method in the granita recipe opposite to make an apple and mint granita.

SAKE AND CUCUMBER GRANITA

MAKES ENOUGH FOR 2 DOZEN OYSTERS

2/3 cucumber (for 125ml cucumber juice)
1 small bunch of fresh mint, leaves picked
10g caster sugar
50ml sake
1 gelatine sheet
25ml mirin
25ml lime juice
a pinch of sea salt

This is handy for making in advance if you're serving oysters for a party. It also makes a lovely palate cleanser between courses. You can use this same granita method to play around with other flavours, such as the apple and mint foam on the previous page.

1. Put the cucumber, mint leaves, sugar and sake in a blender and blitz together. Chill in the fridge for 30 minutes to allow the flavours to marry together, then pass through a fine mesh sieve.
2. Soak the gelatine leaves in a little cold water for 5 minutes.
3. Warm the mirin gently, then add the gelatine, stirring to dissolve. Add the lime juice and a pinch of salt.
4. Transfer to a large freezerproof container or baking tray and put in the freezer for 2–3 hours, stirring or scraping with a fork every 10–15 minutes to give it a slushy texture. Use within 48 hours or freeze for up to a week.

PISTACHIO CRUMBLE

MAKES ABOUT 120G

50g premium-quality shelled green pistachios
50g caster sugar
35g cold unsalted butter
1 tablespoon honey

We serve this with our pig's head fritter and rhubarb purée on page 59 but this nut crumble would pair well with rhubarb-based desserts too.

1. Preheat the oven to 180°C.
2. Put the nuts in the centre of a clean tea towel, cover and break them up with a rolling pin into a rough crumble.
3. Mix together with the sugar, butter and honey, either in a mixer or by hand with a wooden spoon to incorporate. Spread out on a tray and bake in the preheated oven for 15 minutes.
4. Remove from the oven and set aside until ready to use or transfer to a well-sealed container and refrigerate for up to a couple of weeks.

HONEYCOMB CRUMB

MAKES ENOUGH TO GARNISH THE CHOCOLATE PISTACHIO TART ON PAGE 155

100g caster sugar
35g liquid glucose
20g honey
1½ tablespoons water
1 level teaspoon (5g) bread soda

We use this for the chocolate pistachio tart on page 155, but it can be dipped in melted chocolate to make a little petit four or sprinkled over a panna cotta (page 161) or creme brûlée (page 152).

1. Line a baking tray with non-stick baking paper.
2. In a small saucepan over a medium-high heat, combine the sugar, liquid glucose, honey and water and bring it to 160°C (use a sugar thermometer).
3. Whisk in the bread soda and pour the mixture into the lined baking tray. Set aside somewhere cool to chill.
4. Once cold, break it up roughly and transfer to a ziplock bag, where you can use a rolling pin to break it up further. Store in a cool, dry place for up to two weeks if the bag is well-sealed.

INDEX

36-hour slow-braised short rib lasagne 98-9
777 (restaurant) 14

A
Ahessy, Mark 2, 11, 12, 14, 16, 17, 19, 88, 94, 120, 201
almonds
    charred broccoli with smoked almonds, yuzu and pickled chillies 122, 204
    lamb rump and shoulder with baba ganoush, tzatziki and spiced olive sauce 103
Amaretto Sour 161, 188
Andarl Farm 17, 106, 177
apples
    apple and mint foam 43, 212
    apple purée 106, 209
apricots
    apricot purée 57, 116, 209
    sage, apricot and walnut stuffing 132
arancini 50
    lobster and prawn arancini 33, 197
Arnold, Hugo 15
aubergines: baba ganoush 103, 207
avocado purée 36-7

B
baba ganoush 103, 207
bacon
    pea and ham soup 70
    roast chicken supreme with gnocchi, smoked bacon, glazed carrots, peas and chicken jus 92-3, 207
    Wagyu beef and free-range pork meatballs with puttanesca sauce 55
bain-marie 24
baked potato mash 140, 142, 146, 148-9, 203
Balfegó tuna 19, 36-7
ballotine 24
Ballyhoura Mountain Mushrooms 104
Ballymaloe House 14
Banana Mai Tai 156, 188
Bang Café 15
basic gnocchi 202
basil: crispy basil leaves 33, 206
béarnaise 192
    rib-eye steak with béarnaise and beef dripping chips 94-5, 184
béchamel 193
beef *see also* brisket; oxtail; short ribs
    beef and Guinness pie 142-3
    beef dripping chips 94-5, 100, 120
    beef stock 199
    rib-eye steak with béarnaise and beef dripping chips 94-5, 184
    Sunday roast beef 130
    The Old Spot burger 100
    Wagyu beef 16
    Wagyu beef and free-range pork meatballs with puttanesca sauce 55
beetroot gel 104, 211
beignet, oxtail 53, 66, 81, 85, 211
Bentley's 12
bisque
    prawn bisque 108, 196
    lobster bisque 33, 193, 197
black pudding
    pig's head fritter with rhubarb, black pudding and pistachio 59, 88, 204, 213
    pork chops with colcannon, black pudding, apple purée and cider jus 106, 177, 198, 209
    Sneem black pudding 17-18, 59, 106
blood oranges
    Old Spot, The (cocktail) 106, 177
    yogurt panna cotta with blood orange jelly and ginger crumb 161
Bloody Maria 43, 184
Bloody Mary 43, 130, 184
Bloody Mary jelly 43, 212
Blue Blood Bramble 104, 180
bluefin tuna 19
    bluefin tuna with avocado, ponzu, sweet and sour peppers and black sesame 36-7, 177
Bono 7
bourbon: Old-fashioned 95, 184
Bourgogne Aligoté 166
bread
    bread and butter pudding 158
    Guinness brown bread 34, 64, 106, 148-9
brine, how to 25
brisket
    beef brisket 82
    scallops with brisket, celeriac, pickled carrot and quail egg 40, 82, 186
broccoli: charred broccoli with smoked almonds, yuzu and pickled chillies 122, 204
brown sauce, homemade 56-7, 146-7, 194
burger, The Old Spot 100
burger sauce 100
Burns, Kieran 17
butternut squash
    butternut squash risotto with crispy sage and toasted walnuts 50, 179
    gnocchi with squash, goat cheese, pine nuts and crispy sage 116
    pumpkin and ricotta ravioli with crispy sage 46-7
    squash or pumpkin purée 46, 50, 116, 208

C
Cáis na Tíre cheese 21
Carlingford Oyster Company 18
Carrigy, Aoife 15, 30, 33, 34, 43, 47, 70, 143, 152, 155, 158, 161, 163
carrots
    carrot tops 132
    oxtail beignet with carrot, orange and black truffle 53, 66, 81, 85, 211
    pickled carrot and celeriac 40, 69, 204
    roast carrots 132
    roast chicken supreme with gnocchi, smoked bacon, glazed carrots, peas and chicken jus 92-3, 207
cartouche 25
Caruso & Minini Frappello 55
Castello di Volpaia Chianti Classico Riserva 99
Caterway 20
cauliflower cheese 135
Cavanbert cheese 166
cavolo nero, deep-fried 104, 206
celeriac
    celeriac purée 40, 104, 208
    celeriac soup with black truffle 53, 66
    pickled carrot and celeriac 40, 69, 204
    remoulade 54-5
    scallops with brisket, celeriac, pickled carrot and quail egg 40, 82, 186
    venison with black mushroom powder, hazelnut crust, beetroot, celeriac and port jus 104, 198, 199, 206
Celler del Roure 'Safrà' 47
cep gnocchi 116, 202, 209
Chablis Grand Regnard 34
Chapter One 12, 14
Charles Heidsieck Brut Réserve 33
charred broccoli with smoked almonds, yuzu and pickled chillies 122, 204
Château de Cèdre Malbec 143, 155
Château du Breuil Calvados 166
Château Phélan Ségur Saint-Estèphe 147
cheese 21
    Cáis na Tíre cheese 21
    cauliflower cheese 153
    Cavanbert cheese 166
    cheese, crackers, chutney 166
    Comté cheese 21, 166
    Coolea cheese 21
    deep-fried truffled mac 'n' cheese 48
    gnocchi with squash, goat cheese, pine nuts and crispy sage 116

Killeen goat cheese 21, 166
Mont d'Or cheese 166
St Tola cheese 21
storing 166
Wicklow Blue cheese 21, 166
chicken
    chicken and chorizo pie 128, 140, 179
    chicken liver parfait with plum chutney and pickled cucumbers 60, 205, 209
    chicken stock 199
    roast chicken dinner 128, 182
    roast chicken supreme with gnocchi, smoked bacon, glazed carrots, peas and chicken jus 92–3, 207
chillies, pickled 122, 204
chips
    beef dripping chips 94–5, 100, 120
    fish 'n' chips 112
    rib-eye steak with béarnaise and beef dripping chips 94–5, 184
    truffle and Parmesan chips 120
chocolate
    bread and butter pudding 158
    chocolate and pistachio tart 155
    Jaffa cake 162–3
    white chocolate and raspberry crème brûlée 152
chorizo: chicken and chorizo pie 128, 140, 179
chutney
    cheese, crackers, chutney 166
    plum chutney 57, 60, 88, 166, 210
cider jus 198
    pork chops with colcannon, black pudding, apple purée and cider jus 106, 177, 198, 209
clams
    cod with orzo, 'nduja, confit tomato and shellfish 108–9, 179
    how to cook 109
Clarence Hotel 12
Clifford, Michael 14
cocktails 170–1
    Amaretto Sour 161, 188
    Banana Mai Tai 156, 188
    Bloody Maria 43, 184
    Bloody Mary 43, 130, 184
    Blue Blood Bramble 104, 180
    Cucumber Collins 109, 186
    Green Door, The 37, 53, 177
    It's Sunny Somewhere 128, 182
    Kew Garden 43, 182
    Kool and Kurious 115, 180
    non-alcoholic 186
    Old-fashioned 95, 184
    Old Spot, The 106, 177
    One for the Road 188
    Play Safe 186
    Sage Advice 50, 116, 179
    Spicy Lychee 140, 179
cod with orzo, 'nduja, confit tomato and shellfish 108–9, 179
coffee: One for the Road 188
colcannon 106, 177, 198, 203, 209
Comté cheese 21, 166
Conceição, Izzy 1, 23, 37, 43, 48, 53, 55, 59, 60, 93, 95, 99, 100, 106, 109, 112, 115, 130, 155, 156
confit tomato 108–9, 179, 206
Cooke's Café 12, 15
Coolea cheese 21
Cooney, Stephen 2, 7, 13, 22
Corrigan, John 16
Corrigan, Richard 12
crab on toast 30, 182
crackers: cheese, crackers, chutney 166
crème brûlée, white chocolate and raspberry 152
crème fraîche, horseradish 34, 53
crispy basil leaves 33, 206
crispy sage leaves 46, 50, 106, 116, 179, 206
croquettes, ham 56–7, 70, 194
crumb
    ginger crumb 161
    honeycomb crumb 155, 213
    parsley crumb 148–9
cucumber
    Cucumber Collins 109, 186
    cucumber pickle 34, 60, 205
    Green Door, The 37, 53, 177
    Kew Garden 43, 182
    sake and cucumber granita 43, 213
    tzatziki 103, 195
Curley, Róisín 166

D

Dafni Psarades 70
De Selby's 15
deep-fried kale or cavolo nero 104, 206
deep-fried truffled mac 'n' cheese 48
deep-fry, how to 25
defrost, how to 25
dehydrated fruit 171
Devereux, Siobhan 21
Devereux, Willie 21
Dooncastle Oysters 18
dressed oysters 42–3
duck fat roast potatoes 133

E

Eden 15

F

Farrell, Andy 11
Farrell, Colin 126

Farrell, Eamonn 126
Fassbender, Michael 114
Favaro, Beatriz 14
fish 'n' chips 112
fish pie 148–9, 203
foam, apple and mint 43, 212
food and drink pairing 23
Frangelico hazelnut liqueur 158, 188
freeze, how to 25
fritter, pig's head fritter with rhubarb, black pudding and pistachio 59, 88, 204, 213

G

Gallagher, Conrad 12
garlic purée 116, 209
gel
    beetroot gel 104, 211
    orange and ginger gel 53, 211
Gibson, Stephen 14
gin
    Blue Blood Bramble 180
    Cucumber Collins 109, 186
    gin-cured salmon with pickled cucumber and horseradish crème fraîche 34
    Green Door, The 37, 53, 177
    Kool and Kurious 115, 180
    Old Spot, The 106, 177
    Play Safe 186
    Ultimate G&T 34, 60, 93, 174
ginger
    ginger crumb 161
    ginger syrup 211
    orange and ginger gel 53, 211
Gleeson, Domhnall 114
Gleeson, Michael 17
Glendalough Single Grain Madeira Cask Finish 69
gnocchi
    basic gnocchi 92, 116, 202
    cep gnocchi 116, 202, 209
    gnocchi with squash, goat cheese, pine nuts and crispy sage 116
    roast chicken supreme with gnocchi, smoked bacon, glazed carrots, peas and chicken jus 92–3, 207
Golden-Bannon, Ross 15
granita, sake and cucumber 43, 213
gravy, Sunday roast 128, 130, 134, 142, 197, 200
Green Door, The 37, 53, 177
Greywacke Wild Sauvignon Blanc 40
Guinness
    and oysters 43
    beef and Guinness pie 142–3
    Guinness brown bread 34, 64, 106, 148–9

H

ham
  ham croquettes with brown sauce and remoulade 56–7, 70, 194
  ham hock terrine 57, 209
  ham hocks 56, 70, 78
  pea and ham soup 70
Hang Dai 17
Harty Oysters 18
hazelnuts
  Frangelico hazelnut liqueur 158, 188
  venison with black mushroom powder, hazelnut crust, beetroot, celeriac and port jus 104, 198, 199, 206
hearty oxtail soup 69
Heffernan, Dave 20
Hewson, Ali 7
homemade brown sauce 56–7, 146–7, 194
homemade mayonnaise 30, 56, 100, 193
homemade pasta 46, 98, 201
honeycomb crumb 155, 213
Hope Beer
  Hop-On Session IPA 115
  Underdog Pilsner 149
horseradish crème fraîche 34, 53
Hostinariu, Mihaela 1
hotpot, lamb 86, 201

I

ice 171
It's Sunny Somewhere 128, 182

J

Jaffa cake 162–3
jelly
  blood orange jelly 161
  Bloody Mary jelly 43, 212
  yuzu jelly 43, 212
Jimenez, Carlos 7, 13
jus
  chicken jus 92–3
  cider jus 106, 198
  port jus 104, 198, 199
  red wine jus 92, 98, 114, 146, 197, 198, 200

K

kale, deep-fried 104, 206
Kavanagh, Conor 2
Keegan, Ciaran 1
Keelings 20
Kelly, Iara 2
Kelly, Stephen 1, 23, 37, 43, 50, 57, 69, 93, 95, 104, 112, 115, 116, 128, 140, 149, 156, 166
Kew Garden 43, 182
Killeen goat cheese 21, 166
Kinnegar Brewing
  Devil's Backbone Amber Ale 57, 95
  Limeburner Pale Ale 37
  Rustbucket Rye IPA 57, 59
  Scraggy Bay IPA 112
Kool and Kurious 115, 180
Kumeu River Chardonnay 72

L

L'Ecrivain 12, 14, 19
La Casetta Valpolicella Ripasso 130
La Rousse 21
La Stampa 15
lamb
  lamb hotpot 86, 201
  lamb rump and shoulder with baba ganoush, tzatziki and spiced olive sauce 103
  shepherd's pie 146–7, 203
  slow-cooked lamb shoulder 86, 103, 147
lasagne, 36-hour slow-braised short rib 98–9
Little Cress 20
lobster
  how to cook 33
  lobster and prawn arancini 33, 197
  lobster bisque 33, 193, 197
  lobster mayonnaise 193, 197
Louët Feisser, Peter 18
lychee: Spicy Lychee 140, 179

M

mac 'n' cheese, deep-fried truffled 48
Marc Brédif Chenin Blanc Vouvray 93
Martin, Michael 12
Mas Saint-Louis Châteauneuf-du-Pape 103
Maslowski, Lukasz 7, 8
mayonnaise
  homemade mayonnaise 30, 56, 100, 193
  lobster mayonnaise 193, 197
  truffle mayonnaise 193
McBrien, Denise 1, 2, 8, 11, 12–13, 16, 17, 19, 23, 34, 40, 43, 66, 72, 103, 128, 130, 143, 147, 166
McGrath, Dylan 14
McLoughlin, Kate 16
McLoughlin, Pat 16, 94
McLoughlins Butchers 16
McMahon, Linda 'May' 3, 8
McNerney, Barry 7
McNerney, Paul 7
meatballs, Wagyu beef and free-range pork 55
Milestone, Dave 17
Milestone, Diana 17
mint: apple and mint foam 43, 212
Mont d'Or cheese 166
Mount Horrocks 'Cordon Cut' Riesling 152
Muga Rioja 48, 100
Mulcahy, Bruce 14

mushrooms
  cep gnocchi 116, 202, 209
  mushroom duxelles 72, 92, 207
  pickled girolle mushrooms 72, 205
  venison with black mushroom powder, hazelnut crust, beetroot, celeriac and port jus 104, 198, 199, 206
mussels
  how to cook 109
  mussels pil pil 114–15, 179, 180, 186, 197

N

'nduja
  cod with orzo, 'nduja, confit tomato and shellfish 108–9, 179
  Wagyu beef and free-range pork meatballs with puttanesca sauce 55
Nico's 12
Niepoort 10-Year-Old Tawny Port 156

O

O'Buachalla, Conor 126
O'Driscoll, Brian 11
O'Malley, Brian 2, 7, 11
O'Neill, Bríd, 13
O'Sullivan, Peter 17, 18
oil 24
Old-fashioned 95, 184
Old Spot, The (cocktail) 106, 177
Old Spot burger, The 100
olives: spiced olive sauce 86, 103
One for the Road 188
onions
  pickled onion rings 120
  white onion soup with pickled girolles 72
oranges
  Jaffa cake 162–3
  orange and ginger gel 53, 211
  oxtail beignet with carrot, orange and black truffle 53, 66, 81, 85, 211
orzo: cod with orzo, 'nduja, confit tomato and shellfish 108–9, 179
oven temperatures 24
oxtail
  hearty oxtail soup 69
  oxtail beignet with carrot, orange and black truffle 53, 66, 81, 85, 211
  oxtail ragù 69
  slow-braised oxtail 85
oysters 18, 182
  dressed oysters 42–3

P

Palmer, Jane 2
Palmer, Patrick 2
pané, how to 26
panna cotta, yogurt 161
Parmesan: truffle and Parmesan chips 120

parsley
  parsley crumb 148-9
  parsley sauce 193
  smoked almond and parsley crust 103
passionfruit purée 173, 186
pasta
  36-hour slow-braised short rib lasagne 98-9
  deep-fried truffled mac 'n' cheese 48
  homemade pasta 46, 98, 201
  pumpkin and ricotta ravioli with crispy sage 46-7
pastry, suet 140, 142, 201
Peacock Alley 12
peas
  cooking 70
  pea and ham soup 70
  pea purée 112
  roast chicken supreme with gnocchi, smoked bacon, glazed carrots, peas and chicken jus 92-3, 207
peppers, sweet and sour 36-7
Peter Jakob Kühn 'Jakobus' 43, 112
Phelan, Tim 14
Pichet 14
pickles
  cucumber pickle 60, 205
  pickled carrot and celeriac 40, 69, 204
  pickled chillies 122, 204
  pickled girolle mushrooms 72, 205
  pickled onion rings 120
  pickled rhubarb 59, 204
Picollo Ernesto Gavi di Gavi 'Rovereto' 128
Pierre Victoire 15
Pierre White, Marco 12
pies
  beef and Guinness pie 142-3
  chicken and chorizo pie 128, 140, 179
  fish pie 148-9, 203
  shepherd's pie 146-7, 203
pig's head 88
  pig's head fritter with rhubarb, black pudding and pistachio 59, 88, 204, 213
  pig's head terrine 88
pil pil, mussels 114-15, 179, 180, 186, 197
pine nuts: gnocchi with squash, goat cheese, pine nuts and crispy sage 116
pistachio
  chocolate and pistachio tart 155
  pig's head fritter with rhubarb, black pudding and pistachio 59, 88, 204, 213
  pistachio crumble 59, 213
pithivier, how to make 26
Play Safe 186
plum chutney 57, 60, 88, 166, 210
ponzu dressing 36-7
Pop, Alisa 156

pork
  Andarl Farm 17, 106, 177
  pork chops with colcannon, black pudding, apple purée and cider jus 106, 177, 198, 209
  pig's head fritter with rhubarb, black pudding and pistachio 59, 88, 204, 213
  Wagyu beef and free-range pork meatballs with puttanesca sauce 55
pork belly: beef and Guinness pie 142-3
port jus 104, 198, 199
potatoes
  baked potato mash 140, 142, 146, 148-9, 203
  colcannon 106, 177, 198, 203, 209
  duck fat roast potatoes 133
  loaded baked potato skins 203
prawns
  lobster and prawn arancini 33, 197
  prawn bisque 108, 196
  prawn stock 196
pudding
  bread and butter pudding 158
  sticky toffee pudding 156, 188
pumpkin
  pumpkin and ricotta ravioli with crispy sage 46-7
  squash or pumpkin purée 46, 50, 116, 208
purée
  apple purée 106, 209
  apricot purée 57, 116, 209
  avocado purée 36-7
  celeriac purée 40, 104, 208
  garlic purée 116, 209
  passionfruit purée 173, 186
  pea purée 112
  rhubarb purée 59, 210
  squash or pumpkin purée 46, 50, 116, 208
puttanesca sauce 55, 69

Q
quail eggs, confit 40
quenelle 26
Quinta do Noval LBV Port 155

R
raspberry: white chocolate and raspberry crème brûlée 152
ravioli, pumpkin and ricotta with crispy sage 46-7
red wine jus 92, 98, 114, 146, 197, 198, 200
Redmond Fine Foods 20
remoulade 56-7
rhubarb
  pickled rhubarb 59, 204
  pig's head fritter with rhubarb, black pudding and pistachio 59, 88, 204, 213
  rhubarb purée 59, 210

rib-eye steak with béarnaise and beef dripping chips 94-5, 184
ricotta: pumpkin and ricotta ravioli with crispy sage 46-7
Ridgeway Wagyu 16, 100
risotto
  butternut squash risotto with crispy sage and toasted walnuts 50, 179
  lobster and prawn arancini 33, 197
roast carrots 132
roast chicken dinner 128, 182
roast chicken supreme with gnocchi, smoked bacon, glazed carrots, peas and chicken jus 92-3, 207
Roeleveld, Marion 166
rum: Banana Mai Tai 156, 188

S
sage
  crispy sage leaves 46, 50, 106, 116, 179, 206
  Sage Advice 50, 116, 179
  sage, apricot and walnut stuffing 132
sake and cucumber granita 43, 213
salmon: gin-cured salmon with pickled cucumber and horseradish crème fraîche 34
salted caramel syrup 172, 188
sauces
  béarnaise 94-5, 192
  béchamel 98, 193
  cheese sauce 193
  homemade brown sauce 56-7, 146-7, 194
  homemade mayonnaise 30, 56, 100, 193
  parsley sauce 193
  tartar sauce 112, 194
  tzatziki 103, 195
scallops with brisket, celeriac, pickled carrot and quail egg 40, 82, 186
Scúp Gelato 21, 155
sesame: bluefin tuna with avocado, ponzu, sweet and sour peppers and black sesame 36-7
shallots, crispy 34-5
Sheen Falls 14
shellfish
  clams, how to cook 109
  cod with orzo, 'nduja, confit tomato and shellfish 108-9, 179
  lobster and prawn arancini 33, 197
  lobster bisque 33, 193, 197
  lobster mayonnaise 193, 197
  lobster, how to cook 33
  mussels pil pil 114-15, 179, 180, 186, 197
  mussels, how to cook 109
  prawn bisque 108, 196
  prawn stock 196
shepherd's pie 146-7, 203

short ribs
- 36-hour slow-braised short rib lasagne 98–9
- oxtail beignet with carrot, orange and black truffle 53, 66, 81, 85, 211
- pumpkin and ricotta ravioli with crispy sage 46–7
- slow-braised short ribs 81

Silin-Palmer, Pamela 2
slow-braised oxtail 85
slow-braised short ribs 81
slow-cooked lamb shoulder 86, 103, 147
Sneem black pudding 17–18, 59, 106
Sondoa, Tallie 9, 15
soup
- celeriac soup with black truffle 53, 66
- hearty oxtail soup 69
- lobster bisque 33, 193, 197
- pea and ham soup 70
- prawn bisque 108, 196
- white onion soup with pickled girolles 72

Spicy Lychee 140, 179
spirits, infusing 170
squash or pumpkin purée 46, 50, 116, 208
St Tola cheese 21
steak
- cooking times 95
- resting 95
- rib-eye steak with béarnaise and beef dripping chips 94–5, 184

Stephane Ogier Viognier 55
sterilising glass jars and bottles 26
Stewart, Terry 7
sticky toffee pudding 156, 188
stock
- beef stock 199
- chicken stock 199
- prawn stock 196
- venison stock 199

Stonehouse Restaurant, The 14
stuffing, sage, apricot and walnut 132
suet pastry 140, 142, 201
sugar syrup 172
Sunday roasts 127–35
- roast chicken dinner 128, 182
- Sunday roast beef 130
- Sunday roast gravy 128, 130, 134, 142, 197, 200
- timings 127
- tips 127

syrup 171
- ginger syrup 211
- infusing 170
- salted caramel syrup 172, 188
- sugar syrup 172

T
tart, chocolate and pistachio 155
tartar sauce 112, 194
Taste by Dylan McGrath 14

Tea Room, The 12
tequila
- Bloody Maria 43, 184
- infused 170
- Spicy Lychee 140, 179

terrine
- ham hock terrine 57, 209
- pig's head terrine 88

Tiller & Grain 14
timings 24
toast: crab on toast 30, 182
tomatoes: confit tomato 108–9, 179, 206
tostadas, tuna 37
truffles
- celeriac soup with black truffle 53, 66
- deep-fried truffled mac 'n' cheese 48
- oxtail beignet with carrot, orange and black truffle 53, 66, 81, 85, 211
- truffle and Parmesan chips 120
- truffle mayonnaise 193

tuna
- Balfegó tuna 19
- bluefin tuna 19
- bluefin tuna with avocado, ponzu, sweet and sour peppers and black sesame 36–7, 177
- tostadas 37

Tyrrell, Simon 13
tzatziki 103, 195

U
Ultimate G&T 34, 60, 93, 174

V
Valles, Gabo 6
venison 18, 208
- venison stock 199
- venison with black mushroom powder, hazelnut crust, beetroot, celeriac and port jus 104, 198, 199, 206

Viré-Clessé André Bonhomme 66
vodka
- Bloody Mary 184
- It's Sunny Somewhere 128, 182
- Kew Garden 43, 182

W
Wagyu beef 16
- Wagyu beef and free-range pork meatballs with puttanesca sauce 55

Waldron, Brendan 8
walnuts
- butternut squash risotto with crispy sage and toasted walnuts 50, 179
- candied walnuts 50
- sage, apricot and walnut stuffing 132

Walsh, Louis 12
Ward, John 18
Whalley, Ernie 15

whiskey
- One for the Road 188
- Sage Advice 50, 116, 179

white chocolate
- Banana Mai Tai 156, 188
- bread and butter pudding 158
- white chocolate and raspberry crème brûlée 152

white onion soup with pickled girolles 72
Wicklow Blue cheese 21, 166
Wild Irish Game 18
wine
- food and drink pairing 23
- service 22–3

Wine Lab 22
Wishbone, The 15
Wrights of Marino 19

Y
Yellow Spot whiskey 163
yogurt panna cotta with blood orange jelly and ginger crumb 161
Yorkshire puddings 134
yuzu
- charred broccoli with smoked almonds, yuzu and pickled chillies 122, 204
- yuzu jelly 43, 212

ACKNOWLEDGMENTS

WE ARE ALL SO PROUD TO celebrate a decade on Bath Avenue and with that comes a lot of people to thank. I have been here for almost seven years and the welcome and warmth of the area is infectious. Whether it's Linda May, the Mayoress of Bath Avenue, dropping in a dinner of bacon, cabbage, mashed potatoes and parsley sauce to me and Brendan in The Bath during Covid, or Sheila Kavanagh dropping me in tights during my ladder emergency, the sense of community and family is unmatched. It would be impossible to name every guest without leaving someone out so can we please extend a blanket thank you to the local residents, the local businesses and to each visitor from near and far – you all bring us joy every day and we are forever grateful. Our Christmas Eve Club gathers all the families together at 2pm every year, only to be cruelly shown the door by 5.30pm. Our rugby lunches are legendary and securing a place now is almost impossible before the key games: the same people come to every match day and have become like friends. I even have my lucky green dress which all the regulars know I'll be wearing.

We have some of the best suppliers in the food business and our relationships with them are so valued. Thank you Jonathan from Wrights of Marino for taking my emergency Saturday morning call and putting fish in a van to us when you are at sports events with your family. Thank you Kate of McLoughlins for taking my calls days after having your baby because our Sunday roast beef didn't arrive. Thank you John of Ridgeway Farm for allowing Mark to to collect emergency burgers because we didn't order enough. Thank you Rocky of Redmonds for always being a supportive hand. I am sure Stuart in La Rousse regrets giving me his mobile number as I panic call for back-up sourdough and Comté cheese; thank you for always picking up, and for connecting us to producers like Balfegó tuna, Andarl Pork, Carlingford Oyster Company and Wild Irish Game.

Thank you to all our drinks suppliers too, from the breweries and distilleries big and small to the wine importers who work so hard to bring us our world-class range of wines. Simon Tyrrell first opened my eyes to the amazing range of wine he imports over 20 years ago and I still love working with him today, much like Andrew from Morgan Wines, who always has the most delicious wines, which I have listed for over 20 years. Ed in Pembroke Wines is a huge support in sourcing special wines for special guests. Fiona in Le Caveau, Claire in WineLab, Rafa in Vinostito, Jamie in Tindal Wines, Ben in Liberty Wines, Charles in Nomad Wines, Enrico in Grapecircus and Ben in Winemason and Niall in Comans – thank you all for introducing us to your wonderful wines.

Thank you to all the food media and guides who have been kind enough to review us and showcase what we do.

The Old Spot team feels like a family and that is because owners Brian and Stephen make us all feel like an extension of their own families.

We all get to know and care for the O'Malleys and that starts with Brian's parents, Kevin and Annmarie. Annmarie will drop in flowers from the garden and sometimes stay for a glass of Guinness and lunch with a friend. Kevin keeps his steely eyes on our wine list and shares my favourite, Viré-Clessé. Brian's sister Grace donated our coveted round table upstairs when she moved to Sweden with her husband Philip and young family. Brian's brother Eoin, who oversees the Loyola Portugal operation, longs to have our roast chicken when he gets back to Dublin with his wife Lara. Brian's sister Catherine is part of our Christmas Eve Club with her husband Peter and their four boys, and their eldest Hugo enjoyed TY work experience with us this year.

The Cooneys are equally as supportive and proud of what we have achieved. Stephen's mum Sheila would come for dinner with her late husband Garrett Snr and always share a Gordon's Gin & Slimline Schweppes Tonic (in a tall glass please, with no fruit) followed by a nice bottle of red with two perfectly cooked steaks on T14. Sadly, Garrett Snr passed during Christmas 2018; I can still remember my last hug with him at Table 66 after a long Christmas lunch he had with an old friend – and the unexpected hug that Garrett Jnr's son Ben randomly gave me one day at the exact spot. Stephen's brother Garrett and his wife Ellen always feel at home with their young family, and Stephen's brother Kevin and his wife Anna enjoy great family lunches with Sheila and her sister Marie at the head of the table.

The Loyola team is a family and it is a great testament that so many have been with the group for years. Thank you to Aidan Morrissey, Justyna Jurak and James Bowes in our finance head office for taking my weekly (and sometimes daily) calls to keep us on track. While most of us become friends, Brendan Waldron, the general manager of The Bath (and longest-standing Loyola GM of almost 13 years), found his wife Orla Condron, our marketing manager, on a management trip to Portugal in October 2018 and they married in May 2023. Thanks to both, and to all our management team, including Gerry Murphy, Colm Mahon, Sarah Jane O'Rourke, Jane Palmer and Conor Mulligan, who keeps coming back to work in The Bath on match days just to get the buzz. So many staff host special events in The Old Spot, as in our opinion it ticks all the boxes with great atmosphere, great food and great service.

Thank you to my great friend Paul Flynn who first introduced me to Kristin Jensen and helped to get this project off the page. Working with Kristin, Aoife, Ruth and Charlotte on this project has been amazing from the start. Thank you all so much for capturing the essence of The Old Spot, but a special thank you to Aoife Carrigy for the hours and hours you spent in our bar to get what we are about. We are beyond proud of what we have achieved, and we look forward to this book being a bestseller!

Thank you so much to the amazing team we have had over the years and for all the love, kindness and happiness you bring to my everyday. I enjoy coming to work every single day and it is all really because of you.

Thank you to the full team who worked with us during this project, starting with our longest-serving sous chef, Lukasz Maslowski, and Elvis Khupoo, Iara Brennan, Mihaela Hostinariu, Natalie Keegan, Talie Martins, Beatriz Favaro, Stephen Kelly, Luc Munier, Patryk Grzelak, Izzy Conceição, Antonio Carlos, Jake Dimond, Anahi Luna, Annmarie Smith, Carlos Jimenez, Travis Ward, Andrew Hughes, Naiara Passos, Alex Munier, Owen Coyle, Ciaran Keegan, Christopher Kilroy, Keelin Collins, Alisa Pop, Marcezo Britto, Conor O'Buachalla, Eoin Farrelly, Claudia Cespedes, Renan Petrachin, Hazel Higgins, Gabo Vasquez, Dragos Amuraritei, Huseyin Baran, Arthur Williams, Adrian Connor, Zach Chard-Ryan, Mario Epiphanio, Marcezo Silva Britto, Maone Barbosa, Stephen Mallon and Jason Kelly.

A very special thank you to our head chef, Mark Ahessy. I have worked with many head chefs over the years, and I enjoy every single day I come to work with you. You have a unique way of managing the kitchen team and supporting the front of house at the same time. Your passion for The Old Spot is as infectious as mine. I am so proud of doing this cookbook with you, it really is a dream come true for both of us. I'm looking forward to working with you for the next 10 years and I hope we've become lifelong friends.

A huge thank you to my family: my sons Conan, Luc and Alex, my mum and dad, and my sisters and best friends, Emma and Katrina. You have all supported me during my 35-year career in hospitality, which has seen me miss many family events, and you have all stepped in when I needed help with the boys.

Declan Maxwell, Robert Scanlon, Peaches Kemp, Paul and Máire Flynn, Kevin Watson and Keith Gillen, I say it often, but I'll say it again: I'm blessed to have you as friends, but god forbid our WhatsApp group was ever accessed!

My partner Cathal is my confession box, and with a past career in hospitality, he completely gets me. Thank you, my love.

Lastly, I would like to thank Brian and Stephen for giving me the freedom to mind The Old Spot. I genuinely enjoy every day in The Old Spot and I couldn't be luckier. We clicked right from the start. You have both given me the opportunity to run my own business again. Hospitality is a unique industry unlike any other and our job is to mind people and make them feel special on the way in and more importantly on the way out. Thank you.

STARTERS

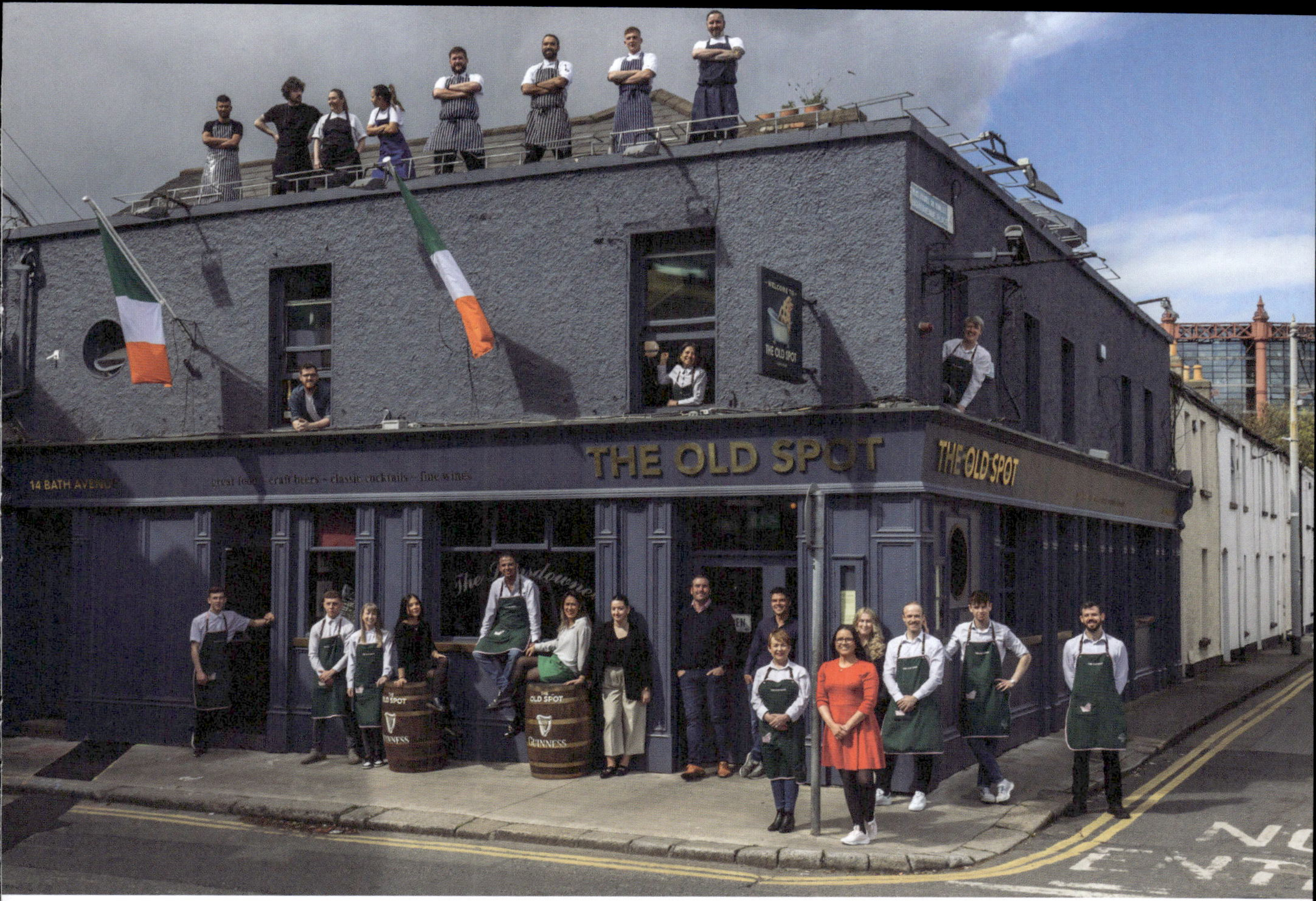
THE OLD SPOT
THE OLD SPOT
great food · craft beers · classic cocktails · fine wines
GUINNESS

PLÁS ASCAILL AN IONNLAIT
BATH AVENUE PLACE 4

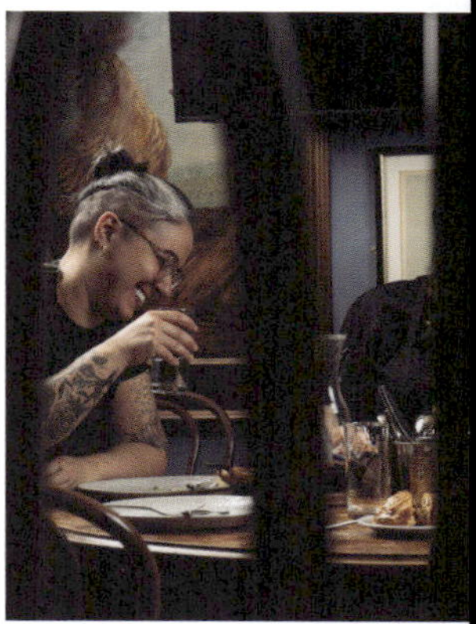

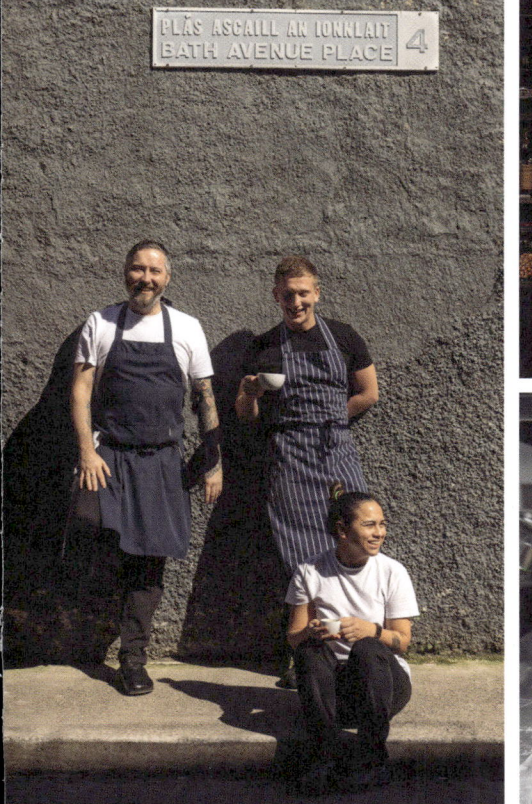

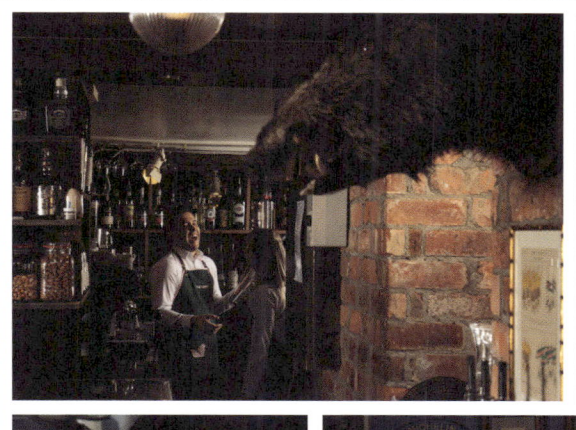

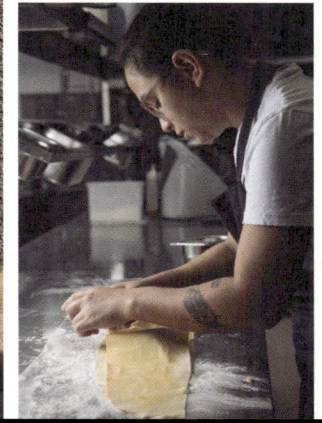

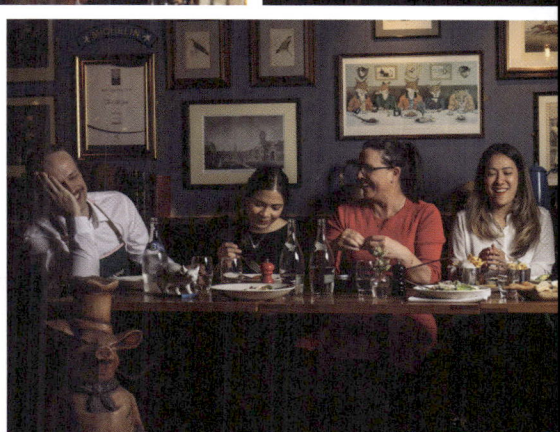

Nine Bean Rows
23 Mountjoy Square
Dublin D01 E0F8
Ireland
@9beanrowsbooks
ninebeanrowsbooks.com

First published 2024
Text © Spot the Pig t/a The Old Spot, 2024
Photography © Ruth Calder-Potts, 2024

ISBN: 978-1-7384795-1-1

Text written by: Aoife Carrigy
Recipes developed by: Mark Ahessy and the chefs at The Old Spot
Editor: Kristin Jensen
Design and layout: grahamthew.com
Food stylist: Charlotte O'Connell, charlotteoconnell.co.uk
Food photographer: Ruth Calder-Potts, ruthcalderpotts.com
Printed by L&C Printing Group, Poland

The paper in this book is produced using pulp from managed forests.

All rights reserved.
No part of this publication may be copied, reproduced or transmitted in any form or by any means without written permission of the publishers.
A CIP catalogue record for this book is available from the British Library.
10 9 8 7 6 5 4 3 2 1